You Are
PSYCHIC

YOU ARE PSYCHIC

IT'S YOUR GIFT — LEARN HOW TO ENHANCE IT

Trish Stevens

BALBOA
PRESS

A DIVISION OF HAY HOUSE

Balboa Press books may be ordered through booksellers or by contacting:

Balboa Press
A Division of Hay House
1663 Liberty Drive
Bloomington, IN 47403
www.balboapress.com.au
1-(877) 407-4847

ISBN: 978-1-4525-0915-0 (sc)
ISBN: 978-1-4525-0916-7 (e)

Because of the dynamic nature of the Internet, any web addresses or links contained in this book may have changed since publication and may no longer be valid. The views expressed in this work are solely those of the author and do not necessarily reflect the views of the publisher, and the publisher hereby disclaims any responsibility for them.

The author of this book does not dispense medical advice or prescribe the use of any technique as a form of treatment for physical, emotional, or medical problems without the advice of a physician, either directly or indirectly. The intent of the author is only to offer information of a general nature to help you in your quest for emotional and spiritual well-being. In the event you use any of the information in this book for yourself, which is your constitutional right, the author and the publisher assume no responsibility for your actions.

Printed in the United States of America

Balboa Press rev. date: 07/08/2013

For Gordon, with love

You have started an exciting journey.
Enjoy developing and enhancing your gift!

Contents

Preface

*D*are to be different. Together, let's have some fun challenging old thought patterns and throwing open doors to new ideas and realities. The work in this book reflects many years of working with spirit, and it explains my views on the universe. My ideas might challenge you, but they will also give you food for thought.

It has been my pleasure for many years to work with the spirit world, a world of people who have passed on from their earth lives to live in the next dimension, many of whom have become guides, teachers, and spiritual masters.

When taking a tour to Brazil in 2009, I was asked by my cousin Glenda to write a book that explained how to do a variety of psychic readings, how to relate to clients, and how to interpret the images and feelings sent by spirit to help. I realized that I also needed to teach people how to connect to their spirit guides, to work with imagery, and to put in the dedicated hours of practice to strengthen their connections and to heighten their abilities.

My spirit teachers have a wonderful sense of humour and great insight into our lives on earth. Many of them have experienced earth lives and now see things from a higher perspective. As a young and inexperienced student, I spent a lot of time meditating, working with energy, and working with a myriad of tools for learning how to read and to help others.

I have had the pleasure of working in Brazil, Chile, Peru, Thailand, and Vanuatu.

Along the way I have had many laughs with my spiritual teachers and have shed a lot of tears for and with those who are suffering from any kind of loss. It took me many years to detach from the emotions, which can overwhelm you in a reading, and I have to admit that I still have problems at times with tears. Earth is a hard school. We choose to have many difficult lessons on this planet, and from these lessons come growth, understanding, empathy, compassion, and love.

This book is designed to help you learn how to become a competent reader, and there are many different types of readings for you to explore—such as flowers, pictures, photographs, feathers, and shells—as you connect to the vibration of the person who has asked for the reading. Readings are fun to explore in a class situation, with friends, and for your own psychic development.

Life is a wonderful journey, and every day is special with the lessons it brings. The good ones fill your day with laughter and a sense of achievement, and the harder ones make you stronger.

I hope that you will work your way through the chapters in this book, developing your psychic and intuitive ability. Connecting with your spiritual guides will open new worlds in your mind and help you to become an effective reader. Readings are fun to practice, and you will work to your own level of understanding, increasing your volume of information and improving your accuracy with practice. As you improve, you will be delighted with the responses from your friends and family as your predictions come to pass. If you find that one method of reading doesn't suit you, then simply move on to the next. There are lots of ideas for you to try. Good luck!

I have started this book with some thoughts and ideas for you to ponder, as well as answering some frequently asked questions. The second half of the book has many exercises for you to train yourself, to do with friends, or to use when teaching classes. Have fun, remember to laugh, and aim at the stars, even if you only hit the chimney tops. Love and blessings to you all.

Acknowledgements

I would like to thank my wonderful husband, Gordon, my children, Kathy and Matthew, and my son-in-law, David for many years of continued love and support and for sharing my time with so many people. I also thank Hilary for adding many years of joy and laughter to our family.

Love and thanks also go to my mother, Betty, for her love, care and constant encouragement. And to my caring and generous brother, David, who designed the book cover and has supported my book through every step of the journey. And to the lovely Honor who has spent endless hours helping me to get this book submitted. Many thanks to everyone else who helped in different ways. Thank you so much.

Love and thanks go to my business partner John for years of support, kindness, and healing, and to Marjorie for her assistance, loyalty, encouragement, and love. A special thank you to Pauline for many years of hospitality and fun times. A big thank-you and love go to my cousin Glenda for suggesting a book with lots of exercises to advance people's psychic development at all stages of their spiritual journey. Also a special mention to Dianne Miles who has supported my business over the years and has become a good friend. I would also like to express my love and gratitude for the invaluable assistance I have received from Robin and Dianne and Leon Ashton.

Thanks also to my students who have become important friends and who have supported my journey, including Jan, Lynda, Barbara, Maggie, Dianne P., Leandra, Stuart, Cindy, Rachel, Steven, Sally and Sarah. Also to all of my South Australian students for many years of dedication and for years of fun and good times.

A heartfelt thanks goes to my friends in Brazil and Chile for enriching my life in so many ways, and to everyone who has attended a seminar or joined me on a tour to sacred places: thank you very much.

Thanks also to Balboa Press for making this book a reality and to everyone there who assisted me in getting this book ready for printing.

To everyone reading this book: I thank you for your support. May your lives be filled with love and many incredible and magical moments.

Introduction

*Y*ou are psychic. Deep down in your heart, you know that these words are true. Everyone has psychic abilities. We have hunches, gut feelings, and premonitions—or we just simply know things. As we develop further, we start to use our gifts of clairvoyance, clairaudience, and clairsentience. We awaken our intuition, and we are ready to learn at a deeper level. We all have the opportunity to develop these skills if we wish to—or to ignore them if the time isn't right for us to make spiritual progress. All will benefit from reading this book if they work with the exercises and meditations. It is exciting to be able to read for others with your heart and soul—and with truth and accuracy.

You are a spiritual being having an earth life in a physical body. You have a strong connection to the spirit world and to your spiritual guides and angels. The exercises in this book will teach you how to work with energy and to strengthen your ability to connect to your guides.

You have chosen your guides to suit your learning in this lifetime: healing guides, teaching guides, and guides for protection and direction on your journey.

Where do we come from? We come from the divine intelligence, which sent out over sixty million divine sparks of consciousness into our universe to enable us to learn and to grow spiritually. Imagine a huge, brilliant sun with white and gold luminous light, sending out sparks into our universe. This would look like firecrackers at night, with a magnificent ball of brilliant light sending out a myriad of glowing sparks, which become monads, and smaller balls of light holding the intelligence of thousands of souls.

Each monad holds the memories of the universe and of the creator. At the head of each monad we find twin souls, who oversee the journey of everyone from their monad, while learning higher lessons themselves.

An example would be the monad that has the twin souls of Saint Germain and Lady Portia. Saint Germain is also the head of the seventh ray, the violet ray of transmutation, and is available to a lot of people to help them to let go of the past, release past lives, and move forward toward enlightenment and awareness. Lady Portia works in the shadowlands with the damaged souls who are struggling to find balance and harmony on the other side. She teaches you how to balance your physical, emotional, mental, and spiritual bodies. She is a very strong and focused woman filled with wisdom and mercy.

We all come from different monads, monads which are comprised of many people and their aspects. Over time, and hundreds of lives, we lose touch with this information. As we have more and more lives and our energy gets heavier, we forget where we have come from and, indeed, why we are here. In our hearts we are yearning for something but have forgotten what it is that is missing from our hearts and our lives. We forget about the unconditional love that is available to all of us at any time; we forget about the love we share with our monad, soulmates, and guides.

We have elected to come to earth to work at strengthening our emotional bodies and to understand duality. We are all striving to find love of self and to love and help others. Each divine spark sent out from the creator, or divine consciousness, created a monad, a base for us to work from and to connect to our higher self and other aspects. Each monad sends out soul groups. Imagine the huge sun sending out basketballs of light called *monads*, and each basketball or monad sending out twelve oranges called *soul groups*.

Can you picture the monad, a large ball of light sending out twelve smaller balls of light called soul groups?

Each soul group creates a base, it is from here that we travel to earth and back for our lessons. As we have many lessons on this beautiful planet, we come and go from here lots of times. Each time, in our early incarnations, our energy gets heavier, and as we work with the lessons from the lower chakras, we may become negative in our outlook. This may cause us to become materialistic and selfish, controlling and angry. If we move into the positive aspect of these energies, we are self-empowered, stable, creative, and honourable. If we pass the lessons presented at these levels, we move on to higher lessons. This takes many lifetimes.

Each soul group—and there are twelve soul groups connected to one monad—has at least twelve personalities that are sent out to work on earth or on other dimensions. At the head of the soul group, we have our higher self, who reflects divine intelligence and is our mentor for every earth journey.

You are one of these personalities. Each time we come to earth, it is with the intention of improving ourselves and redefining our personalities. We strive to work with sound virtues like unconditional love, tolerance, patience, understanding, and fairness.

These personalities have many archetypal patterns with which to work and extend their knowledge. It is a huge picture, but we are all still connected to the source—to our creator, to our twin souls who supervise our monad, and to our higher self who is the mentor of our individual soul group—giving us access to all knowledge when we are ready to learn. As students of life, we will at some stage connect to our spirit guides and to our higher selves to receive information, advice, and guidance. We are never alone. Our guides are always around us, loving and encouraging us.

Are you psychic? Of course, you are! You are a wonderful spiritual being filled with joyfulness, tenderness, and inspiration. You are a co-creator of your life and your world. You have access to all information; you have the ability to connect to guidance and inner truth; and you can work with good teachers on earth who are eager to offer you assistance. When the time is right for you, you will learn how to meditate and to work with the spiritual discipline required to work with your spiritual teachers as they take you through sets of lessons. You need a few minutes a day, and then, when you are ready, you will start building this time up to ten minutes, then twenty minutes, then thirty minutes. You will come to enjoy this special time with your guides and teachers and look forward to the lessons they bring.

We are part of the huge family called humanity. We are connected at some level to everyone and everything on earth. We are here to love and to live through both harmony and strife. We are here to help each other and to be kind and compassionate toward those less fortunate than ourselves.

Unfortunately, we have forgotten our connections to each other, and in the place of love and kindness, we have created jealousy, envy, bitterness, anger, worry, stress, doubt, fear, and violence. In so doing, we have created an emptiness within our hearts.

We have come to learn through separation from both the source and each other, but it is now time to step into spiritual maturity, to be the leaders who help others find their way home and to work always with kindness, truth, and integrity.

Very often I am asked the question, "Why do I feel empty inside?"

Many people experience inner loneliness that they try to fill by going on shopping trips, buying lots of things to fill the cupboards and wardrobes but not the heart. They rack up horrendous bills on their credit cards, but they do not feel any better. Then they need to work long hours or two jobs to pay the bills, and the only small way this helps is in keeping the person out of the house, where they might have been even lonelier.

They may go to lots of parties, running from place to place, trying to fill the emptiness with drugs, alcohol, noise, and dancing, but at the end of the night they leave alone and may even feel worse—or they go home with someone for sex, still trying to fill the void. With the early morning light, they still feel alone. The sex was fun in the moment, but the connection and experience, if not heartfelt, soon fades into feelings of disappointment.

Some try to fill the void with love from a partner. This is a wonderful experience, but if you do not love and approve of yourself, you will still feel empty. You cannot fill the heart of another and help to make them feel special if you do not love yourself. You will still be feeling the "lack" in your own heart. If you do not feel worthy of true love, you will do something to test your relationship and maybe lose it.

The time is coming when people will realize that they first need to fill the gap with self-love and confidence. All of us need to know that we are never truly alone, that we are at all times connected to the universe and to everyone and everything—on this planet and off.

We are continually supported by our spirit guides, so it is up to us to connect through meditation or quiet times. We all need to be able to spend comfortable times in the silence with our own positive thoughts. Positive affirmations are a wonderful tool for lifting your energies and helping you feel at peace with yourself. We are on an exciting journey of self-discovery through divine communication and self-love.

Younger souls thrive on the loud noise, continuous parties, or the hustle and bustle of city life. They look outside of themselves to feel alive, but they eventually reach a stage where they notice the inner loneliness. They can't bear to be alone, travel alone, holiday alone, or even spend a night at home alone. They spend, spend, spend—sometimes to buy friendship—but are not yet ready to realize they must look within for their answers.

It is very important to be able to spend time alone with your thoughts, to sit in the silence and follow the path of your breath, to still the body and reconnect to your inner self. Drugs and alcohol may create a different reality for people who are hurting, but this is a downward spiral that leads to even more loneliness and ill health.

There comes a time when people start to question their lives. Is there more? Why am I still feeling so lonely when I have been out all weekend?

They start to ask other people about the feeling of loneliness, and at this stage they generally start to look within for their answers. They may start to read empowering books, join mediation groups, or ask questions of those who have walked this path before them. They will realize that they are showing the world a false front, and indeed they are presenting a false front to themselves.

It is time to change their thought patterns, to prevent depression, to drop the victim mentality and the "poor-me" syndrome and make positive change. They could start work on their self-esteem, attend courses to raise their confidence, join groups that have lots of positive energy and good ideas to share, and stop themselves each time they want to complain, instead giving thanks for the good things in their lives. Bit by bit, their energy will start to change, and they will feel a difference. There is nothing like a funny movie or book to lighten the mood and thoughts.

We all need to learn how to set some boundaries and say no. Practice some phrases if this is difficult for you to do. Some suggestions would be: "I am not available at that time" or "I am unable to commit to that date." Be firm and definite with your tone, and people will take notice of what you are saying.

Speak to others the way you like to be spoken to. I heard a couple arguing, being verbally abusive toward each other, and then the phone rang and the lady spoke with a sugary sweet tone to the caller. It amazed me that the caller received the courtesy and the husband—the person she should love most on this planet after herself—copped the rough edge of her tongue and complete disrespect.

How can you respect yourself if you are screaming, losing control of your emotions? How do you speak to your partner? How do you speak to your parents, children, friends, and clients? Which face do you present to the world? Is it a changing face because you still do not live true to yourself? Is the person you present at work different from the person your parents see, the person your partner sees, and the person you know you truly are in your heart? It is a challenge to continually improve your communication skills and to develop the mature virtues of tact and diplomacy.

Your true self is the one that you will be able to show to everyone. Your intent comes from your heart, so you no longer work and live with jealousy, resentment, and bitterness. You no longer need a huge house, designer clothes, and expensive wine to impress your friends. If you have these things, it is because they make your heart sing. Your heart is filled with love, and love knows no boundaries and is non-judgemental. If you have the trappings of wealth, you might like to share your bounty with those who are still struggling. They are a part of you, a part that may at some stage need the help that you are able to give. In each soul group we have a variety of people and a variety of challenges and difficulties. If it is your turn to have wealth, be generous with it. If it is your turn to listen and grow through the advice or experiences of others, be open to it. It might be your turn to be humble, generous, helpful, or caring. Know that these qualities bring the appropriate lessons.

You are a student of life, blessed to live and be part of the earth experiment. Along the way we make many mistakes and have lots of opportunities to laugh in retrospect at some of the decisions we have made.

With love and compassion, warmth and true desire, you can make this world a better place. Share your bounty and care for everyone. You do not know why others make the decisions they do; just know that it is their right to do so. If they want your help, they will ask for it, and you can give freely of your time and abundance to them.

True knowledge involves the balancing of the right and left brain, the logic and reason balanced with the gut feelings and intuition. When we are in balance, we have access to clairvoyance, clairaudience, clairsentience, and higher knowing. Only then can we turn the knowledge into wisdom and be a mentor on earth.

Teach others how to speak to you; teach others how to treat you. It is up to you to create the boundaries of respect and courtesy. Always communicate with others with dignity and tact, leading the way with responsibility and integrity, and fill your true potential as a spiritual being on earth. Add joy and humour into your day. Make someone smile and laugh as you enjoy every new experience.

Be proud of every decision you make. When making life-changing decisions, ask yourself who will be hurt by your behaviour. If I take my best friend's husband/wife, can I build my happiness on someone else's unhappiness? Moral decisions bring the hardest karmic lessons: don't do to others anything you do not want done to you. If you are not proud of the decisions you have made, maybe you need to think again. If you are ashamed of your actions or words, you will feel heat in your body, your face will flush, and you have a need to look down. This is the energy of shame. Let your body talk to you and help you to make sound progress. Be happy to learn from any mistakes that you make and then move on to the next set of lessons.

If you are unhappy at work, you have options: retrain, look for another job, and see if you can improve relationships at work by changing your own attitude toward someone. Make your enemy into your friend, and in so doing, you will change the attitude of that person and make life better for both of you.

People we do not like bring us the biggest lessons. They make us dig deep into our inner selves to find the answers that will make us proud of all decisions we make. We all know the little inner voice, which, when we are about to do something stupid, says to us, "Don't do that. Go home now." And we all know how to ignore this guidance and go ahead with our shopping, drinking, etc. It is time now to connect to your higher self or guide and take the good advice offered.

It is a good idea in this day and age to do some computer training. It is available for the young through school, but for many of us it is a complete mystery. There are lots of good classes available, and you may meet new friends or go on to use your new skill in a profitable way. You can educate yourself through the wonderful articles that are available or catch up with people from your past through social media sites. Classes of all kinds are available, and the opportunities are boundless for new hobbies and extending your skills. By moving yourself forward into this age of technology, you stay in touch with those around you.

Be progressive in all areas of your life. Don't let the energy around you grow stagnant, or you will become resentful of those who are moving forward. Keep your life interesting and challenging. You are a student of life, a person lucky enough to be here on earth at this changing time to experience the rapid growth of your soul and to help others.

If it is time to open your heart to compassion, there are many lessons connected to the heart chakra. You may like to learn counselling, first aid, or age care; do some babysitting for a tired mum; help a family in distress; or take your children to a park for the sheer joy of hearing them laugh. Think about your life. What do you do to connect to your heart energies, to bring joy and happiness into your life and into the lives of others? Think about who you can forgive so that you can move forward into new energy.

Spending time in nature brings a wonderful feeling of peace. Rain forests have many hidden wonders: filtered light, all shades of green to rest your eyes, and earthy smells to ground you and provide you with precious peace that rejuvenates you.

Much joy comes from being in service to others. Can you cook a spare meal for someone who lives on their own? Wash a floor for a sick friend? Take someone shopping, if they do not drive? These simple things mean so much to others, and they promote your own journey into the higher energies.

You could take time in the morning to say your affirmations in the shower, during your early morning walk, as you are eating breakfast, or on your way to work on public transport.

You could try to find some time in the morning or evening, or maybe when you are sitting in the garden, to meditate. It is so easy. Just go into the silence and follow the exercises in this book—or simply enjoy the silence. Ask some questions and wait to see if they are answered for you. Answers may pop up anytime. Just be aware that hints are often answers, unexpected words from others, and even a stranger may be there simply to pass on a message.

You might like to make a list of things that you like about yourself—to build your confidence and self-esteem. Everyone has something. Start with at least ten things, and add to your list daily. Suggestions would be:

- I appreciate my lovely eyes.
- I love my hair; it is silky, and it makes me feel special.
- I am a wonderful person, filled with self-love and love for others.
- I am opening to spiritual advice.
- I am connected to my guide daily.
- I meditate very well; I love the silence.
- I have a pretty smile.
- I am passionate and free.
- I am happy and filled with love.
- I am generous with my time and energy.
- I am open to positive change.
- I seek the truth and internal guidance.
- I have good dress sense.
- I am awakening to my spiritual gifts.
- I am making positive changes in my life.
- I am happy, and I am creating magic in my life.
- I am filled with enthusiasm and confidence.
- I have a great sense of humour.

The list is endless, but you should easily be able to find about one hundred to get started with. Read your list from top to bottom every day, and add to it to build your confidence.

In your private moments, you may like to send out love and healing to people you care about. Ask for blessings to be sent to those in need of help or support. Truly care from the bottom of your soul, if someone is in distress, and always ask spirit people to help you.

Look into the mirror and list your good points. Include all of the things you have to offer as a partner, son/daughter, mother/father, friend, employee, teammate, or humanitarian. It is exciting to think about our good qualities, as we tend to be able to find our negative traits easier than our positive ones.

Think about something that happened in your past and review that time. If it was a happy experience, enjoy that feeling. If it was not, then see it with clearer, older eyes, and you may find new lessons in the episode that you did not see when you were younger. Let go of old hurts and move forward. It is so important to be able to forgive yourself, as well as others.

Become your own best friend; find pleasure in being by yourself and connecting to your heart. It is okay to be by yourself. If you live alone, it is because you need special time to nurture yourself. Think about the wonderful things you can do to make your daily experience special. Know that you are a wonderful spiritual being having an earth life. Know that you have chosen this life and the people to interact with.

Think of something you can do each day to improve your life or the way you feel about yourself. Then find a bigger task, once a week, that will lift your confidence. Notice how your body feels when you do something nice for yourself or someone else. The divine flame in your heart flares and sends warmth through your heart and soul. It is a wonderful feeling.

A sense of humour will make a huge difference to your life. Try not to be too serious. Lighten up and learn to laugh at yourself when you do something silly or make a small mistake. We are only human, and sometimes we just simply get it wrong. Embarrassing moments give you lots of laughs for years to come.

I once walked around the Gold Coast airport, waiting with my husband for a plane, and I noticed that a lot of people were looking at me. I thought it was because I am a fairly big person, so I was commiserating with myself because the people were rude. However, I saw the situation in a different light when an old lady stepped up to me and said, "My dear, I don't think you know it, but your dress is tucked up into the back of your pants, and everyone is looking at your bottom." Yipe!

Enjoy reading many spiritual books from the library. It is fun to learn, to question the information, and to challenge yourself to talk to your guides about the things you have read.

CHAPTER 1

Where Is Our Spiritual Home?

Over time, many star systems, planets, and galaxies—with many different levels of consciousness—were formed in our universe.

In our earth lives, we reside on earth in the third dimension. However, we are spiritual beings who, between earth lives, live in the fourth dimension.

This is our true spiritual home, and it is to this level that we and our loved ones return between incarnations on earth. Here we are happy, working hard toward spiritual growth, and continually learning.

It is here that we arrange each earth journey, the lessons we need to learn, and the karma we need to release, extending our knowledge and turning it into wisdom. We are assisted in doing this by a council or group of guides who have our best interests at heart.

We do not all reside at the same level in the fourth dimension, as there are many levels. We tend in our early lives to want to return to the groups we are comfortable in—sometimes religious, sometimes cultural—where we find stability. We are always excited to be reunited with members of our soul group, where we have very special bonds.

People who have been violent on earth will find, when they pass over, that they are in the lower fourth dimension. Here they will receive help to balance their energy fields and to reflect on the life just lived. Helpers who work in this area are trained and compassionate, willing to spend their time helping troubled souls. These souls are unhappy, angry, and in need of help, and this will be given to them. Healing and advancement is available to all of us.

Those who are struggling in their earth lives with greed, spite, materialism, lack of forgiveness, dishonesty, unreliability, etc., will find when they pass over that they see life from a different perspective. These souls will make new choices that will assist their journey to enlightenment in future trips to earth.

Often these souls find themselves living in a communal situation in the fourth dimension or in a home with older souls to care for them and to advise them. When shown their lives at the karmic board, they often have a need to make positive changes, and there is always someone there to help them change their ideas and to motivate them into wanting a better life next time.

For those who are genuine, kind, and caring, the level will be higher. As we tend to come with our spiritual groups to earth, we will be reunited with our loved ones, whichever side of the veil we are on—third or fourth dimension.

Soul groups come into the third dimension together to help and support their individual growth and the growth of their soul group. As the understanding and knowing becomes a lot higher, they are aware of raising the level for their monad as well.

As we raise our own level of consciousness, we leave behind us the need to judge others, and we use this energy to discern so that we may be of assistance.

When we are ready to come to earth, we choose our life plan, set up our sacred earth contract, and come here as babies. We elect to forget everything about the fourth dimension, as we would struggle with homesickness and long for those we have left behind, and memories of our past lives would confuse the issue of whom we should love in the here and now.

There seems to be a part of us that yearns for our spiritual home and the loved ones we leave behind. You can be taken in your mind to your spiritual home through meditation.

You can be connected to your loved ones in the next dimension through the wonderful work of spiritual mediums.

CHAPTER 2

Earth

Our earth is also a monad—a living, sentient being—that provides us all with a home, shelter, water, food, and a lovely place to learn our lessons. We are asked at all times to treat the earth with respect, as she is a living, breathing being. We are a warring people, and we attempt to destroy our planet through wars, famine, and negative thoughts, which create tsunamis, earthquakes, tidal waves, and other natural disasters. Big companies work hard to amass a fortune while destroying our gorgeous planet. Oil slicks above the surface destroy our bird life and then move under the ocean and keep travelling until they destroy enormous numbers of creatures who make their home in the sea. We throw our rubbish into the oceans and leak sewage and chemicals into this formerly pristine environment.

How would this glorious planet look without modern man? Can you imagine it as it was meant to be—clean, fresh, and unspoilt by greed? The exquisite Amazon, the lungs of the earth, is filled with wildlife and unusual wild and leafy vegetation, with light filtering through the large green leaves of majestic trees. There is the sound of silence, broken only by the calls of birds as they move around in the deep foliage and fly majestically in the sky.

Imagine animals in many countries scurrying back and forth: the stealth of the big cats, the ponderous journey of the elephants, the towering giraffes, the family of wise wolves—and bright and fragile butterflies adding a splash of colour to this beautiful place.

The rivers on earth run deep and wide, some filled with white water, rapids, and waterfalls. Other waterways slowly meander through fields between scenic banks lined with tall trees, and most are filled with crystal-clear water as they move toward sparkling seas. We would see golden beaches with glistening sand and towering, snow-capped mountains, untouched in all of their glory. Once we had all this. Will we have it again, or will we destroy such splendour, thoughtless in our quest for money?

Mining rips the earth apart, destroying the natural balance. We clear vegetation from the land, creating dust bowls and promoting famine. We block and pollute the waterways and drop litter all over the face of the earth. We kill our wildlife for pleasure; it is a very poor thing to brag about killing a defenceless animal. We fight over religion. Is this what a kind creator planned for us? Or were we given free will to worship and live in the manner best suited to our spiritual development? Maybe if we treated each other as we would like to be treated, if we spoke to everyone with respect and acted with honour and dignity, the world would be a better place to bring up the next generation. We are their mentors. What are we teaching those who follow in our footsteps?

As we become more enlightened, it is up to each and every one of us to help with cleaning up our planet, recycling, using our veggie scraps as mulch, and doing anything at all to persuade others to join our cause and keep the earth beautiful. For those who walk regularly, there is opportunity to pick up rubbish and dispose of it. Not all souls on earth are at the same level of understanding, so it is up to those who are working ahead to take extra responsibility and to help in any way possible. There is time to teach our children to respect the earth and to work hard to help her with her daily struggles.

What is happening now with the earth? She is shifting. It is the end of an era. She is lifting her vibrations and moving her consciousness toward the fourth dimension. She is shuddering, trying to slough off the negativity that is encasing and smothering her. It is the only way she can fight back to let us know that "enough is enough." We should love the planet that houses us and provides everything we need to survive. It gives a home to many different animals and millions of varieties of trees and plants. The plants provide us with medicine to keep us healthy, and many of our illnesses are created by our negative thought patterns in this or previous lifetimes.

We have reached the end of the fifth sub-root race, and this energy has brought many negative thoughts and happenings to the surface for us to make changes. We need to work through the current energy and be masters of our destiny into the new root race.

It is time for the people of earth to take responsibility for their problems, to stop passing the blame to others, and to recognize that to move forward they need to become problem-solvers instead of being apathetic. We have the power with our own thoughts to improve our lives, to turn away much of the illness that holds us back, and to make this planet the very special school it is meant to be. Let's work together and be co-creators of our new world.

Every year heralds big changes of consciousness for those who are ready to connect to their spiritual guidance.

As spiritual readers you will have the opportunity to help the earth by making positive suggestions to your clients, helping them to sort out their resentments and move forward. It is important to suggest several choices to people, not to try to run their lives for them. There are limitless opportunities, and sometimes it just takes someone to make suggestions.

You could hand out paperwork with ideas for cleaning up our planet, and suggestions for alternative cleaning products. Many people will make the change if you do the work and provide the names of companies who are working toward cleaning up our lovely planet.

If the readers united, we would make a big difference.

The overseer of the earth experiment is Kanat Sumara, who works with a group of Sumaras to help us, to protect us, and at times to convince the universe that we are doing the best we can. We are on shaky ground, both literally and metaphysically, and it is time for us all to step up and be of service.

CHAPTER 3

Spiritual Masters

*E*arth is blessed to work with the guidance of many spiritual masters. Spiritual masters have completed the lessons we are currently struggling with. They have learned to master themselves and have passed the initiations, which enables them to work at that level of attainment.

Some of these people have walked the earth journey and some have not, but they are all filled with compassion for humanity.

Seven of these masters work on rays of learning and light. It is their job to oversee the lessons and to help when needed, and they are assisted by many spiritual guides and the angelic realm.

There may be occasions when spiritual masters come here from other dimensions to spend periods of time on earth. An example of this would be Saint Germain, who is said to have lived on earth as Christopher Columbus. They usually oversee from afar, sending in their helpers to assist us.

They encourage us to work with truth and integrity. They ask us to be kind and compassionate and to treat others with dignity and respect. They promote peace and harmony, nonviolence, dignity, and non-discrimination. Their jobs involve global planning, helping governments, and helping to break down the control held by large corporations.

Some of them encourage us to look after the environment and take care of the wildlife that has been sent here to enhance our planet. They send energy to lift the vibrations of earth—and healing energy for all of us. They work at a galactic level, helping the universe.

The masters responsible for working on the seven rays are very special, and they have a total commitment to our earth and our personal journeys. You can meditate to work with these masters and to receive information from them.

First Ray: El Morya

El Morya is said to have incarnated as King Arthur. He focuses on the throat chakra, teaching us to speak with divine truth and integrity. He promotes dedication, tolerance, and patience and asks that we surrender our will to the will of the creator. When we are in harmony with the creator, our lives are on-track and we are in service to spirit. He promotes faith and self-empowerment, courage and justice. People on this ray are often in a position of power, and they learn how to empower others without arrogance or the need for control. This is the blue ray.

Second Ray: Lord Lanto/Kuthumi

Lord Lanto had many early incarnations in ancient societies and in China. Lord Lanto encourages us to connect our heart chakras to our crown chakras and to meditate and work with the yellow flame of wisdom. The crown chakra is further opened after the heart chakra has extended. He asks us to use wisdom in our everyday lives, to look outside of normal thinking, and to be open always to new ideas. He encourages us to treat others as we would like to be treated. This ray carries the love vibration and encourages wisdom. Love is the answer to many of the problems on earth. This is the yellow ray.

Master Kuthumi is now a world teacher with connections to the second ray. He asks us to find the peace in our hearts by letting go of any illusions and to share our bounty with honour, not resentment. It is important that we all respect ourselves and everyone around us and that we work toward releasing any emotional pain so we can move into a better future.

Third Ray: Paul the Venetian

Paul the Venetian was a famous painter on earth. In one incarnation, he took his skills to Peru and worked with colours that would not fade. Some examples of his work are in the museum in Santiago. It was a pleasure to go there and to see his vibrant artwork, still perfect after all these years.

He asks us all to bring colour back into our lives, to go away from the world of beige and to live with glorious colour. He wants us to take notice of the colours in nature—the many varied shades of green, the ever-changing blues of the sky and the oceans, and the brilliant colours of the birds that enhance our lives with their beauty. He asks that we be aware, every day of our lives, of the healing colours that surround us and promote our growth. We choose coloured clothes to enhance our healing without giving it any thought. From now on, pay attention to which colours you are drawn to wear. Colour is a gateway to healing. This is the pink ray.

Fourth Ray: Serapis Bey

Master Serapis Bey incarnated as a high priest in Atlantis and in Egypt. The qualities he embodies are purity, harmony, and self-discipline. He is a tough taskmaster but is much loved by his students. He enjoys working with people who are almost ready for ascension, who have given up selfish pleasures and are filled with love for the creator. He works on the white ray.

Fifth Ray: Hilarion

This is the ray of healing and science. The master of this ray is *Hilarion*. Hilarion has had many lives as a mystic and healer on earth. He works with doctors, nurses, specialists, technicians, scientists, ministers, and healers. He raises the spirits of those souls who have become disheartened or have gone off their spiritual paths through hard times. He promotes truth and clarity. He asks that we work with love and understanding and let go of anything that is holding us back on our journey. He is the master that healers call on to help them with their work. This is the emerald-green ray.

Sixth Ray: Lady Nada

This ray is held by *Lady Nada*, spiritual partner of Sananda, who held the ray before her. She is the only lady master to hold a ray. She has had many past lives as a lawyer or priestess. She works to help us to find devotion, justice, and freedom in our lives. She promotes our psychic abilities and intuition and encourages us all to heal our inner child and to soften in the current energies. She wants us to love ourselves and then be of service to others who are struggling. She likes to work with ritual and initiations and is endlessly encouraging with those she works with. This is the ruby ray.

Seventh Ray: Saint Germain

Saint Germain has had many earth lives, including Christopher Columbus, Count St. Germain, and many more. He encourages us to be in extended family groups, to help and support each other through the coming changes and times. Stepping away from your individual journey a little—to work in balance and harmony with likeminded people—is a step forward on your journey. He encourages transmutation and moving forward. He asks us to look at the times we lapse into a victim mentality and to make changes that promote our growth. This is the violet ray.

Lady Portia

Lady Portia is known for her work with the souls who have lost their way and who are in need of strong healing and direction. Endlessly patient, she works tirelessly to help these souls. At times the Lady Portia works with her twin flame, Saint Germain, to help the people of earth to heal and move forward.

Lady Serena

Lady Serena works as an ambassador and counsellor at high levels and also brings her skills to earth to help with negotiating, when required. The United Nations and all governments could benefit from her fair and just words.

Some of My Guides

William is my doorkeeper when I am doing mediumship. *Arturius* is a special friend and guide who has followed my earth journey and has been a constant support to me. *Geronimo* is a shaman warrior who comes to me with grounding and good common sense. He is a master of the weather and has for years tried to teach me to work with the weather patterns as well as the cosmic rays of healing to lift the vibrations on earth. I might need a few more lifetimes to work this one out.

I am fortunate enough to work with several spirit guides, teachers, and healers. Their advice has always been accurate and insightful, and I consider myself lucky to be a student. My love and appreciation go to all of those guides mentioned—and to the ones I have not listed but have had the pleasure of working with.

Many teachers say that they come from other planetary systems to help us learn astrology, healing, and science, to help us find the path home, or just to love and support us. We are also supported and helped by guides from the fourth and fifth dimensions, who care for us and promote a need for answers.

Your relatives who have passed over still love you and help keep you safe on your journey. They help to lift your psychic and intuitive energies and give you answers, which you need to listen carefully to. They are with you during your special times—birthdays, celebrations, weddings, and the births of lovely new souls into your family—and also in the darker moments when you need to be loved and comforted.

When you work in this field, you no longer need proven facts; the answers simply sit correctly in your soul. Always talk to your spiritual guides about the information you are hearing or reading, and they will be pleased to discuss it with you. Be open to new information, but also be discerning.

You all have a special guide who loves you and looks after you while you are on earth. You all have guardian angels to light your pathway, to comfort and care for you. You are psychic. You are an esoteric student. Have faith in yourself and in your guides, and you will be surprised at what you can achieve. Everything comes from a warm and open heart. Open up to your intuition. Take the time to learn how to meditate and to connect to the inner realms.

There are many books filled with information about the spiritual masters who assist earth, and I would recommend that you would enjoy reading them and learning more about these special, caring, and selfless souls.

CHAPTER 4

Readings

There are many different ways of raising your vibration before a reading. I like to have some quiet time to open myself to the incoming energy.

When we sit with clients to do psychic readings, we are reading from their auras. We are all surrounded by our auras. Our auras consist of our energy bodies, which vibrate faster than our heavy physical bodies. Those who can see auras know that we are surrounded by fast-moving, beautiful colours. It is from there that we conduct our readings.

You can ask your guides to move closer and help you to draw the future and helpful information from your client's aura.

Readings are often challenging and are very interesting. Ask spirit for information that will be of great value to your clients, and then offer suggestions and alternative pathways for clients to consider. It is important to be honest and respectful to those who come to you, as they are trusting you to work with truth and accuracy. You will have the privilege of reading for many interesting people over the years. You will not be a fortune teller, and you may never read about huge wins, marrying the rich and famous, or being left a castle in Scotland. It would be incorrect to make choices for others, so be careful to simply offer suggestions. People will always choose the pathway that is correct for them at any given time, as each pathway leads to their current lessons. Readings may incorporate numerology, palmistry, tarot, clairvoyance, clairaudience, clairsentience, counselling, and helping people to release the past so they can move forward to the next lesson. Mediumship may also play a part in your readings, giving some of you the opportunity to help bereaved people. There are times when past-life therapy is also involved. Put your heart and soul into your readings, and you will find that you may be of service to many people.

My pathway is wonderful and exciting. I have the opportunity to meet many lovely people and to learn from them. I have help from my spirit guides and the angelic realm—in particular, Archangel Rafael, who has a wicked sense of humour and incredible healing abilities and who is very patient with his humble student. This kind of help is available to everyone, as your guides are ready to assist you.

You will be continually developing the skills of clairvoyance, clairaudience, and clairsentience. The training with your higher self and guides will be ongoing for your entire lifetime. Some of you will have these skills from a young age, while others will need to build them as they learn and improve. Stay focused and positive and enjoy every minute of this wonderful life.

When I am doing a reading, there are times when I can clearly hear comments from spirit. Other times, I work with pictures. For example, a picture of Mickey Mouse means the man's name is Michael. An emu tells me that someone is about to stick their neck out in a situation, or that they are a sticky beak and need to be careful with words concerning others. If I am shown a chicken, it means that I should stop clucking and get on with the job. So, yes, spirit does have a great sense of humour.

There is so much doubt when we start working. Are the voices or thoughts real? They sound like our own thoughts. Sometimes they sound like we are just talking to ourselves but with distinctive grammar that may not be our normal way of expressing ourselves.

My messages from spirit are very positive and encouraging. In readings, I have learned over the years to trust my spiritual helpers. I have never had spirit helpers who swear or give me negative feelings. I call on my spiritual helper before every reading or healing, and I call on my spiritual teachers before I teach a class or seminar. I have complete trust that their help will be there for me. It is always thrilling when I do mediumship, when people connect to their loved ones who have passed and are keen to send messages of love and confirmation of life after death. We all connect differently; there is no right or wrong. Your spirit helper will help you in the manner that suits you.

We have many undiscovered talents and abilities. Through simple exercises and practice, we can open ourselves to the world of intuition and inner vision. My aim throughout this book is to show you the exercises I do when working either as a spiritual reader or teacher.

Some people are fortunate enough to be born with these skills available to them. I believe this is based on past life experiences, as we all come to this awakening when the time is right for us. Do we have the right to organize the lives of others? No, we don't. But I do believe we can be very helpful in offering suggestions.

Everyone has the potential to open up to their intuition. For most of us, it is there on a day-to-day basis. Through meditation, hard work, and mind exercises, we can strengthen our abilities. For some it is easier, depending on the level of their soul's advancement. At any time in our lives we can choose a pathway of love, light, and healing. We should never judge another; it may not be their turn yet to open to the light.

It is important in a relationship that you have the freedom to be a serious esoteric student. Your partner does not have to walk this pathway with you, although it is easier if he or she does. If not, you just need enough freedom to learn. Try to find a friend who will be eager to listen to your discoveries and to join you in the exercises to connect to spirit world.

It is pointless to be jealous of other people's abilities, as these are always dependent on past lives and on the amount of time they put into their own development in this lifetime. You can, however, learn from them and advance your development by using their exercises and breath work on a regular basis. Keep a light heart. This is not rocket science. It is simply tuning in to extra abilities to help yourself and others. You can do it. This is who you really are—an energetic being having an earth life—and you have the ability to serve and to heal. You just need to develop it.

Work and learn with a sense of humour. You will need it, as spirit people like to have fun, and it is easier in your everyday life if you can have a laugh. Laugh with others and make them laugh.

The energy of laughter and happiness is infectious, so share it around. While it is important to be serious in your undertaking, you can still use your sense of humour to lighten dark moments and to ease the tougher lessons. Laughter raises your vibrations, and in turn, you become a better psychic.

CHAPTER 5

Sacred Places

On Earth

*T*he wonderful feeling of peace and tranquillity you will feel in meditation will often be present on earth in places like the ruins of Machu Picchu, a meditation pyramid in the Amazon, the Temple of Goodwill in Brasilia, in Brazil, in a church, in the outback of Australia, sitting on the beach, in a garden, or in a house filled with love.

There are many fabulous spiritual tours available at the moment. I suggest you save for this special project and enjoy every minute of learning in these magnificent places. You will make new friends and lift your awareness, and with some teachers you will have the opportunity to clear past lives. Small tours have always been a special part of our lives, and we thank everyone who has joined us in the past.

I have spent many years in the Australian outback, where the sunsets are brilliant and awe-inspiring, and the open spaces invite you to open your heart and learn in the silence. The wide-open spaces, the incredible terrain, and the opportunity to be alone without being lonely are very special. The aboriginal people of all races have a special connection to the land and a deeper understanding of its aliveness.

Become familiar with this energy of silence. Find some favourite places to meditate and to enjoy your connection to the divine. You could try walking on a beach, climbing a mountain or hill and sitting in the silence, or being on a boat with the gentleness of the waves lulling you into a peaceful place in your mind.

Some of my favourite places to sit and absorb this energy include Mount Tamborine in Queensland, the Gawler Ranges in South Australia, and the Dom Bosco Temple in Brasilia, where the stained-glass windows reflect blues and indigos into the temple. The calming, steadying, peaceful energy that abounds here wraps you with love and acceptance. For anyone travelling to Brazil, it is a truly lovely experience to visit this scared place. And while you are in Brasilia, you may also like to visit the famous Temple of Goodwill. This non-denominational temple welcomes people from all over the world. You are invited to walk on the scared spiral, saying prayers or affirmations, giving your problems to the universe, and walking out with the faith that you have been heard and that your wishes will be granted if at all possible.

Gardens and parklands provide everyone with a sacred space to sit and rest and meditate. They are so lovely and serene, and it is especially wonderful if there is a water feature to calm your emotions. You could find a special place on the beach; at sunset or sunrise would be excellent, so you can enjoy the grounding and restful energies.

Younger souls make a lot of noise, speak loudly, and need to be entertained so they are not bored. Shouting and bullying shatters the energy and can really intimidate people. My spiritual teacher refers to shouting as a lack of self-control, with the person shouting having the major problem in the communication. There is often a need to be right and to talk over the top of others. As you grow, you find the value in quiet times and in being by yourself to experience the power of the inner worlds. You learn the value of listening and of quietly sharing your knowledge.

Meditation is not difficult, and it is very calming. Relax in the energy and be at peace. You may prefer creative visualization, forming mind pictures as you work. There are many wonderful recordings out there for you to work with.

Breathing exercises help you to work with higher vibrations. Mantras and chants are also relaxing and peaceful. You might like to try different mantras to calm your mind.

Sacred Space in Meditation

In our mediations we go into a beautiful area that we create, which is called our *sacred space*. It can be the same place every time, a place you reinvent every now and then with gardens, etc., or it can be a different place, e.g., a secluded beach, a mountain, a fairy circle of mushrooms, or a sacred temple. It is always your choice of where you go to work. There are several small meditations in this book for you to try. Where have you found sacred spaces? Would you recognize this energy anywhere in this world?

Areas with Heavy and Negative Energy

Heavy, negative energy can be found where people are violent, addicted, deeply unhappy, angry, arguing continuously, and living in fear and doubt. There are many negative emotions and circumstances that promote heavy energy, including guilt, road rage, stress, physical abuse, emotional abuse, control over others, verbal abuse, sexual abuse, rape, and murder.

This energy is also very easy to recognize. Sometimes you can walk into a room that has very heavy energy after an argument. It is very uncomfortable, and you quickly make excuses to leave. Have you been anywhere where you sensed the danger and left immediately?

We are all very sensitive to energy, and we become more so as we mature spiritually and our inner senses develop.

Cleansing a Room

It would be wise to be aware of the different ways to cleanse a room in which an argument has occurred. Cleanse with a sage stick, lavender oil, symbols, or by running white light through your body and out of your hands as you say positive affirmations.

It is sensible to cleanse a room before you do readings in it so that you are working with pure white light and positive vibrations.

Meditation is one of our greatest tools to lift our energy and to connect to our spirit guides and helpers. You can make a sacred place in your home with soft lighting and a comfortable chair, by playing soft music or just enjoying the silence. Make this your special time, and ask not to be disturbed. In a meditation room, the energy will be cleansed and higher.

It is important for all of us to have a sacred place, either here on earth or in our meditations, to use and enjoy. We all need to be in the silence at times and to connect to spirit. Regular, even, and connected breathing also helps us to move our consciousness to a higher place.

If you are lucky enough to go to the sacred sites on earth, you will have wonderful experiences, as your energy will lift and you will feel closer to the source.

CHAPTER 6

Your Higher Self

Your higher self is both masculine and feminine and is the totality of all of its personalities. Imagine, if you can, your higher self, who holds all records of your lives and the lives of your aspects, guiding you on your journey. You are aspiring to learn and to send this information back to your higher self. You are also working on connecting to your higher self so that you can gain information to help you with your lessons. This is a two-way street.

They are always there for you, and they ask guides and angels to help you. If you imagine that there are twelve aspects that make up the totality of your higher self, then you are never alone. There are eleven others of you out there, learning and maybe even connecting physically with you in this lifetime.

Some people you meet certainly feel very familiar. These people are your soulmates, and yes, you do have more than one soulmate.

If you truly marry a soulmate, then you marry someone from your soul group who has the same higher self. You also interact with others from your monad and from other monads.

Your higher self speaks to you on regular basis and asks questions to stimulate your thought patterns. Wanting to know what you think or feel and how you intend to handle your problems, encouraging you at all times to go deeper with your thinking.

Your higher self asks that you respect yourself at all times and see the beauty of the world in which you live—and the beauty in the souls who inhabit this world with you—and to search for balance, harmony, and peace, learning from everyone you meet and turning that knowledge into wisdom.

The higher self tells us that we should strive for inner knowing, balancing the energy of logic with intuition. There is an exercise in this book to help you to connect to your higher self.

You are part of your higher self, an aspect of your higher self. There are other aspects of your higher self as well. Imagine that you are just one personality sent out by the higher self to learn and grow through many different experiences. We will work with the theory that the higher self sends out twelve aspects of itself. Each aspect has its own personality, traits, abilities, and skills. Each aspect has its own challenges to conquer and negatives to turn into positives. Each aspect has its own past, present, and future lives.

Each personality chooses its own lessons in every lifetime that way the higher self learns faster. And you are part of your higher self.

Some of your aspects are on earth, some are in spirit, and some may be on other planets or in other dimensions, learning different lessons. Just because we cannot see people on other planets does not mean that life does not exist there. Possibly they are in another dimension out of our earth vision.

The universe is our playground, not just Mother Earth. Be open to learn esoterically the things that you will not learn through science. These are things that are not based on earth facts, and yet you know with every cell in your body that they are true.

You are important, and your study is important, as is the amount of love you send out from your heart to everyone you know and to the earth.

Archetypes: Soul Patterns of Behaviour

All of us have a collection of archetypes to teach us how to handle our earth lives and relate to others, to give us strength and courage, and, most importantly, to teach us how to love ourselves and others. Each one of our personal archetypes asks different questions, has a different outlook on the life we are leading, and has different challenges for us.

There are many reasons that people seek readings. We will explore many questions and discuss how you can help people feel valued and reconnect them to their guide systems.

CHAPTER 7

Your Spirit Guides

Our guides come from many levels or dimensions. We live in the third dimension. There are many more dimensions, and each dimension is divided into planes of existence. Spirit guides come from the dimensions where they are best suited to help you on your journey. If you are an esoteric teacher working from the heart chakra, your guides could come from the upper levels of the fourth dimension, the fifth dimension, or higher.

They may be people we have had earlier lives with, and sometimes our friends stay behind to assist us to catch up.

They may be family members who have passed over. Often we have a spirit family who oversee our lives and give helpful suggestions. They come with kindness, love, care, and endless encouragement. When I am privileged to speak to these people in spirit, they always impress on me how much they love their earth family. Some come to me to pass on their regrets or their apologies, but most just send their love.

The angelic realm also works closely with us: hundreds of angles willing to help and advise us as we move up the pathway of life.

There are spiritual teachers who come to teach us through certain parts of our lives. We may be about to work our way through a tough lesson, and they come in for a few weeks or months to assist.

We have a guide with us from the day we arrive on earth. Sometimes our guides will stay with us for our entire lifetime, and sometimes they will step out for a while as we work with another guide, if we have something in particular to learn.

Some of our guides come from our other soul aspects who are not on earth with us this time. They watch, help, and encourage us to get things right, as they also benefit when we grow spiritually.

Sometimes we learn faster than expected, which again will bring in different guides. If we repeat a lesson over and over because we simply don't absorb it, our guides patiently support us through this.

Our guides can only teach us to their levels of advancement, which is why we have different guides for different things.

We often have healing guides who assist us with our day-to-day health, helping us through major illnesses or operations, or they are teaching us to be healing guides. When we work with clients, we hear and work with our guides thoughts, as they give us ideas and solutions to problems we may encounter when working with our own health issues or the issues of others. These guides study at a much higher level than we do, and have many answers for us.

We have artistic guides who give us inspiration and fresh ideas to work with. These guides work with artists, sculptors, authors, playwrights, and all those in the artistic fields. We have music guides who help in all aspects of singing, writing, producing, and insights. We have guides who oversee our daily lives and who promote our spiritual awareness.

When guides speak to us, we may hear them by clairaudient means, or we may get impressions, thoughts that do not match our own. Sometimes we clearly understand that the person is speaking to us with an accent, or we may have the impression of a well-educated person or the rougher speech of someone who had a harder life on earth. You will experience thought patterns and information that you do not have. You will learn to trust the information and to pass it on with accuracy.

Your guidance may come through pictures. This is called *clairvoyance*. Sometimes the pictures will show something accurately; other times they will be symbols, colours, or references to something that has happened to you, so you can use your intuition to sort out the message. Take your time and get it right.

You will experience strong feelings called *clairsentience*. Pull those feelings into your heart and see how they sit with you.

Spirit will also touch your face, arms, or shoulders, and they send goosebumps up your arms and face and sometimes down your legs. For me, this is validation of a home run. At times you just know the information is correct, and you have no doubt whatsoever in your mind that it is so.

Angels

We also have guidance from the angelic realm. Many angels spend time with us, making suggestions, helping with healing, and giving us comfort when we need it. We can talk to them in our meditations, walking in the garden or at any time. They are thrilled to think that we have the faith and acceptance to speak to them. There are healing angels, artistic and creative angels, lifetime angels, and environmental angels.

Archangels

The archangels oversee the angels and work at a higher level. They work with governments, large corporations, and the education systems of all races and countries.

The archangels are there for us for the bigger problems, especially helping us to release blockages and to forgive those who have hurt us. By refusing to forgive, we hold back our own journeys.

In time to come, we will all be clairvoyant. We are raising our vibrations continuously toward this, and more and more people are asking the important questions: Why are we here? What is our purpose? Who can we help? How can I be the best person I can be? At this point in our journey, we are all intuitive, so work with this energy to improve your life and the lives of others.

Earth Angels

Earth angels often appear in our lives when we are in danger. These kind souls step up to the mark and help us when we need it most.

Many years ago, we lived in Mannum, South Australia, a small town on the banks of the River Murray. One Saturday when my husband, Gordon, was working late, my daughter Kathy and I went in to meet him as he packed up for the day. As we were walking to meet him, we noticed a little boy about two years of age walking along the bank of the river.

We greeted my husband and went on chatting, but when my husband looked up, the little one was nowhere in sight. Gordon ran to the river, and sure enough, he had fallen in. Gordon reached in and pulled him out. Dripping wet and clearly very upset, the little boy was crying and hanging on to Gordon as he stood with him, comforting him.

A couple of minutes later, the mother arrived, snatched the child, glared at my husband, and left in a hurry. He didn't have time to explain, and she never asked why her child was soaking wet. I think that was Gordon's opportunity to pay back some karma by saving that tiny tot's life. The chances of us all standing where we could see the river bank were slight, as usually Kathy and I walked in through the front door. Had we done so, the child would have drowned. I hope he went on to have a happy and bright future, even if he doesn't remember the man who saved him.

A similar thing happened at Murray Bridge on the banks of the Murray River when we were picnicking with my parents. A couple of young boys about eight years of age were playing on the bank. My father was strolling around, looking at the ducks and chatting to my young daughter, when one of the boys fell in and the other one took off. My father, who couldn't swim a stroke, was very strong, so he went quickly to the edge and pulled the boy out as he was going down for the third time. We were all some distance away, and Gordon started to run to the water's edge, but by the time he arrived, the boy had been saved. He was very lucky that Dad was so near. The boy looked at Dad and promptly left, good manners abandoned when stress and fear took over.

Years later, I saw my brother David saved by an earth angel. My friend Pauline, his daughter Nicole, and Gordon and I were standing a long way back from a boat ramp, chatting, while my brother was helping his friend John put his very large boat onto the boat trailer. David was standing right in the path of the boat, where he was temporarily out of John's vision, when the boat suddenly moved very quickly. As it did, a man came out of nowhere and shouted for John to stop. The boat came to rest on David's chest, pinning David between the bow of the boat and the trailer, leaving bruises, a cracked sternum, and quite a bit of pain for a few weeks. Two inches further, and I would have witnessed his death. The man simply vanished before David could thank him—and before we got close enough to see him properly. Loading the boat was something David helped John to do lots of times, both before and after this incident, without any problems. Again I felt a karmic debt in action at the appearance of David's earth angel.

My husband is one of my earth angels, and he is generous in sharing my time with many people. He makes me cups of tea in the middle of the night when I am talking to distressed people. He is endlessly kind to everyone who comes into our lives and is of constant support to me.

Another example of an earth angel would be my business partner John, who for many years, nearly every day, channelled reiki to me to help me overcome illness—and then to improve my fitness and health after the illness. Thank you, John.

I know a lady who lost her child to manslaughter, almost destroying the family with sorrow and heartache. Her very special friend Barbara cooked the family dinner for weeks, dropping off her basket of goodies every day—with love and sometimes a bottle of wine. This is a wonderful example of a humble woman who is, to me and to this family, an earth angel. She is a lady who works tirelessly for her own family, babysitting, looking after three elderly people for many years and a sick husband, and often working in her son's business. I greatly admire you, Barbara.

I have a lovely young friend who works in the mining industry. After many industrious years driving a truck, she decided to up the ante, and with eager anticipation, she learned to be a trainer. The pride she felt in herself was palatable, as she has always considered herself to be very ordinary.

One day on the truck, a short time after completing her training, she was training a person who noticed that she had missed something. With great glee, he told her that he would be reporting her, which resulted in her being stood down from work.

While alone and suffering for her mistake, an older man came to fix the smoke detector in her room. Seeing her distress, he went off and came back with essential oil drops to calm and settle her. Their ensuing conversation lifted her spirits, and the oils worked to make her feel less stressed. This older man was her earth angel on a day when she really needed one.

Some people come into our lives to help, and others create karma and drama, having a need to be noticed. Unfortunately, my friend has lost her nerve and will not be going back to teaching, a loss for many students who will not have the benefit of this girl's patience, humbleness, and helpfulness. What she did learn through this experience was to appreciate the kindness of a stranger who touched her life briefly and to learn how much everyone at work likes and supports her.

I have another friend who has fostered over one hundred children in this lifetime, as well as bringing up three of her own children. After experiencing a very difficult childhood herself, she worked tirelessly with her husband to help other children, to keep them safe and help them feel loved. Marjorie, you are an example to us all.

CHAPTER 8

Things You Will Need to Know as a Reader

Everyone on earth has free will. A good reader will respect this and will only offer choices that the client may not have considered. The client will take the option that suits them at the current stage of their spiritual journey. When we leave the spiritual realms to have an earth experience, we set a few opportune meetings and lessons for ourselves; the rest is left for us to sort out on arrival on this wonderful planet.

It is incorrect to think that your life is fully planned and that you are stuck in any way. You will always have the benefit of free will, so use it wisely and be the best person you can be. A sense of humour is a great asset on earth. If you can laugh at yourself, you can quickly pick yourself up and get on with the business of life.

It is very important to engage your heart when you are doing a reading. If you read from the bottom chakras, you will not get the depth and compassion that you can achieve from opening and engaging the upper chakras. Read from the heart, and you will be very helpful and kind. Read to someone else the way you would like someone to read for you.

When people arrive for a reading, they often feel vulnerable and worried. They come to you when they are in need of important answers. They are looking for someone who is willing to be of helpful service, someone who has a good reputation for accuracy and compassion. They are looking for good answers, not criticism.

It is very important that you do not tell your clients what they must do; you are not the conductor of anyone else's life. You are simply a guidepost, pointing out the different directions, giving positive choices, and then stepping back.

Those who are good students and learn their lessons fast may sidestep some of the lessons and move forward faster. If we get stuck in negativity, our lessons may be repeated several times until we find our way into clear energy.

Hurting others will hold back our progress, as will lies, jealousy, envy, deceit, resentment, bitterness, and refusal to forgive.

We all have crossroads in our lives, when sound moral decisions will be of huge advantage to us. We have to make these decisions with a true heart, and it may be that we step away from what we think we want in order to get to a better place.

Readings are always a challenge, but they present many opportunities to help. It would be intrusive to insist that your clients follow your ideas, as your ideas are only suggestions for them to consider before making important choices. Spirit says to make your suggestions clear, to offer good choices and then step out of the way.

There are people on earth who are true wisdom-keepers and who have a clear channel back to the realms of spirit. The advice from these people is invaluable, but again I say it is always the choice of the client to take or leave the advice.

From our clients' point of view, they have the choice of doggedly going down the same pathway to get what they think they want. Or they can reflect on their choices, one of which will give enormous growth on a spiritual path. As always, it is their choice.

Many times after clients have left me, I know that they will choose the most difficult path—one based on finances, security, being looked after, or choosing someone who is good-looking, charming, and smooth-talking. Even when I see their heartache ahead, I acknowledge their right to choose what they think they want and deserve.

Do these people come back again for another reading? Usually they do. However, they generally know what they want me to say, and once again they will take little advice unless it coincides with their own desires. Such is life. I suggest that you do as I do and send them love, light, and healing in your nightly prayers.

Can Anyone Read?

The answer is yes—if they are open to psychic readings or mediumship.

You will normally attract to you the people you can help the most. They are attracted to the light in your heart chakra and would therefore benefit a lot from some sound suggestions.

It is up to clients to discern who is the right reader for them at any stage of their journey on earth.

Will You Always Have the Answers?

No, you will not. You will have the information that spirit sees fit to give you at any given time. If you do not know the answer, be honest and say so.

There will be times when your clients are faced with discernment lessons, and you can only give some options. The decisions must be theirs. Discernment lessons are based on moral choices that will be offered, and there are always crossroads, with several options ahead.

Confidentiality

Confidentiality is very important. What you see and hear in a reading must remain with you and not be fodder for gossip. A breach in confidentiality often comes when young readers are excited because their readings have come right, so they have the need to tell everyone how good they are. This is usually based on excitement rather than a desire to hurt others. Resist this urge and get a good name for yourself. I find it is easier to read for only one partner in a relationship; then there isn't a conflict of interest.

It is often a good idea to put the reading out of your mind; the information wasn't for you, so just let it go.

It is also important not to talk about who has been to you for a reading, as this is also confidential information. You may find yourself reading for a large variety of people over the years, and each and every one of them is entitled to confidentiality.

Rich or poor, good-looking or not, we are all on the journey of the soul, looking to build love of self and love for others.

Spirit Calling

In some readings you will receive information from relatives who have passed over to the other side. This is called mediumship. They will probably send messages of love, forgiveness, and birthday or anniversary blessings. Ask for the name of the person who is sending the message. If you do not get the name, ask for a description of the person, the manner of death, or something only known to the family to validate your message.

Tears

Some people will be tearful when they receive messages from their loved ones. Be kind and considerate, and take your time. It is an exciting time for them to receive this information.

Give your clients time to compose themselves. Often they come to you wanting to believe but not feeling too sure about the process or the validity of your work. We all have to start somewhere with our belief system. Be encouraging and helpful as you see someone step onto the spiritual journey home.

Laughter

Laughter is also a method for releasing tight emotions and coping with the information someone is being given. People with a sense of humour are delightful to read for, and nervous laughter can help a person to unwind and relax with you.

The Difference between a Good Reading and a Bad Reading

A tongue-in-cheek answer here would be that a good reading tells the client exactly what they want to hear!

My real answer would be that a good reading is based on heart energies. Readers respect clients and do their best to give out information that will offer choices to help clients improve their lives, or they channel departed relatives to help clients heal after bereavement. Mediumship readings always require validation—and huge amounts of compassion, accuracy, and kindness.

At all times, read with integrity for the highest good of your client. Be kind, thoughtful, and honest. Remember that your client will remember every word you say, so be exact with your grammar, wording, and content.

Spontaneous Readings

I was walking through a mall many years ago, when a lady's voice asked me to go into the jewellery shop and tell her daughter happy birthday from her mum. I hesitated, as I really didn't want to go in. The shop was fairly full, so I had an excuse not to. While I stood there, trying to tell the mother no, that I would not be going in, the shop emptied, and she said, "There you are. In you go."

So I went into the shop and gave the young lady her message. She asked how I knew, and I told her that her mother had told me. "Couldn't have!" she replied. "She is dead."

"Yes, she is," I said. "I am a medium, and she asked me to pass the message on to you." It was indeed her birthday, and I had the opportunity to pass on a couple of messages from her much-loved mum.

CHAPTER 9

Relationships

Some of the most common questions are about relationships. Here are some guidelines and some things for you to consider when reading about this topic.

Currently, about 52 percent of first marriages and 69 percent of second marriages end in divorce. Some suggestions and fresh ideas might be advantageous when reading for people with marriage difficulties.

A good relationship is based on love, respect, trust, faithfulness, truth, integrity, common goals, personal space, and quality time spent together—and recognizing that both partners take turns at being the flower or the gardener.

If a client is in a dysfunctional relationship, it is not the job of the reader to decide who should or shouldn't stay together. You will often know the most likely answer, but you are obliged to give dual pathways to your clients if possible. Let them keep their power by making their own decisions. With so many factors causing the breakdowns, you can offer some suggestions, solutions, names of counsellors, and the benefit of your experiences working with people for many years. Have the names and addresses of good marriage counsellors to hand out, or take some counselling courses to help you with your work.

Infidelity

Why do people stray? Why do they make life-time commitments then fail to find happiness?

The answer probably has to do with the emptiness within and the inability to understand that, first and foremost, we all need to love ourselves.

When a person places their heart into someone else's hands, the recipient many panic over the enormous responsibility. How can one person know what another person needs to find inner happiness? It is our individual responsibility to fill our hearts with love, warmth, and compassion; and then, with our tanks full, we can embrace the love being shared with us. Some of us don't really know what love from the heart chakra involves. I would suggest some of the following as a good starting point: passion, attraction, love, trust, reliability, honesty, respect, tact and diplomacy in speech, attentive listening without interruption, kindness, caring, patience, co-creation of partners' lives, nurture, responsibility, and so on.

We have to realize that a relationship is not just about a fancy wedding, where the bride looks wonderful and has very high expectations. It is about the fifty years that follow, through sickness and health, through financial difficulties and negative thoughts and actions. Financial problems may also feature for many people.

Can a relationship survive infidelity? What does it take?

This problem can be handled in several ways. One way involves lots of discussion and true forgiveness, accepting the fact that one's partner made a mistake—either through curiosity or attraction to a partner from another lifetime. A person could be dealing with physical attraction, which burns very brightly for a short amount of time.

Infidelity may be caused by fights at home, lack of affection and sex, tiredness, or insufficient special times. Maybe the spark has died out and a person feels their time is up, or they may have elected to come together only for a while to finish something off or to tackle hard lessons.

Good communication is paramount to having a good relationship. Take time out of your busy life to talk and to listen. Take it in turns so you aren't just hearing one point of view;

both partners should offer suggestions for helping to mend the relationship.

Speak to each other with respect and kind words. You are mature adults looking for answers.

Situations a Reader Will Face

Players

There will always be people who are happy to play in their lower chakras, needing new challenges and hidden affairs. Their souls will remain empty, but their egos will run riot, forever searching but not realizing what they are looking for.

These people usually choose good-looking partners to have an affair with. They may like to make love in places where they might be caught—as part of the thrill. They often choose a friend of their partner's and are impressed with themselves if they get away with this for some time. They get high on the chase, on the thrill, but after a while they realize that they are not connected through the heart chakra, and again they feel empty.

Perpetual players brag about how they can get anyone they want with sweet words and promises built mostly on lies. They brag about how good they are in bed and how attractive they are to the opposite sex. They believe they can get anyone they want, and maybe they can—but can they keep them? Can they find heartfelt love when they are betraying someone? My grandmother used to say that self-praise is no recommendation. That sounds right, don't you think? People who act a certain way to win a lover can only keep up this act for a limited amount of time before their true personality sneaks through to the surface. Many who rush into a relationship find this to be true. Another old saying is: what they will do *with* you, they will do *to* you. Again, it's probably true.

Refusal to Let Go

So many people find themselves alone because their partners move on and they are left on their own. They feel a terrible insecurity and are unable to let go of what they thought they had.

You simply cannot make someone love you. If your partner does not want to be with you, it is time to move on. Maybe you have been given some time alone to strengthen your self-love so you'll be ready to step up next time. Time spent on your own can be very valuable for your spiritual growth and the strengthening of your self-esteem. Forgiveness is a very important lesson in this instance. It will allow you to be free to let go and to love again—both yourself and another person.

It is embarrassing and harmful to your own self-esteem to continually pursue someone who has no interest in you.

Letting Go

Look at your situation as a lesson, and see what you have learned about yourself. Often one person grows faster than the other. Or you might have decided in spirit to be together for only so many years, and when you come to earth you forget this and find the separation very difficult.

While you will still experience the sadness and pain at the end of a relationship, you will eventually be in a position to step back and learn from it. It is important to be able to confide in someone and talk out your feelings, as this will help you to move on. Before you go to sleep at night, try to send the person who has left you love and blessings, softening the energy between you. Time, as always, is a great healer.

Abusers

Most abusers are very needy people. They draw very heavily on their partners' energy, time, and resources. As the relationship progresses, so does the amount of abuse.

Abused people often accept the blame for the abuse they are receiving, believing that they have made their partner angry or that they deserved the abuse because the situation was their own fault. If you accept abuse without walking away, it will happen again and again with increasing regularity.

As abusers lack self-esteem, they build their power by taking power from their partners. They may need to know where their partners are at all times, whom they have been with, and exactly what time they will get home. Abusers will check phone bills, text messages, and emails, always wanting to know whom a partner is speaking to and what was said. They may coerce their partners away from friends and family with words like, "They don't understand you like I do" or "They don't love you like I do."

As the abuse increases, victims may find that they have a gap between themselves and their families. This makes it hard to go home or to tell even a best friend what is happening. The shame does not belong to the victim. It falls squarely on the abuser.

These people are controllers. They correct your errors and tell you how to do mundane jobs—like hanging the washing on the line, putting extra salt in a meal, sweeping, vacuuming, ironing, and shopping—until your confidence is slowly eroded away. They tell you what you can and can't do. When you are going out without them, they may phone you while you are out. You will be told when you are expected home and what you can and cannot say outside of the house. You could find that your clothes are chosen for you or that you are instructed on how to do your hair and how much makeup you can use, as abusers are often very jealous and angry people.

Is this love and affection? They read your emails, open your mail, listen to your phone calls, and stand outside your bedroom door while you are having a private conversation. These little things are signs that you are being abused.

Early in a relationship you may consider this to be love and affection. Some make this mistake because they are so grateful that someone "loves" them. They are proud of the attention and may even feel superior to their friends in the beginning. However, all of this changes. As time goes by, you realize that you are now living a very restricted lifestyle: your friends stop visiting or phoning to take you out, your family withdraws so they don't get you into trouble, and it becomes harder to maintain any personal space and dignity. The honeyed words cease to thrill you, as they are followed by jealousy and control.

Eventually the trips to the hospital start. Your lies ("I slipped and fell," "I fell down the stairs," or "I tripped over the dog") are not fooling anyone, and you will probably not do anything to change your situation until you are really hurt—or someone steps in and rescues you.

Be responsible for your life and the way you are treated. Set some strong boundaries and get the help you need to find your personal freedom and self-esteem. It is not a good journey to be a victim. Face your lessons and make the changes you need to make. There is always someone out there to help you to move forward.

Recognizing an Abuser

Look at a person's family. Abusive traits often pass down through a family as learned behaviour. Is the mother manipulative? Is she bossy? Does she have to know everything? Is the father someone you do not care to be with? Is he bad-tempered, cynical, sarcastic, or overbearing? Does your partner tell stories of beatings, starving, or cruelty? Are they still scared of a parent? Bullies can be cowards when dealing with someone mentally or physically stronger than themselves.

Have you and your partner discussed discipline for your own children, and are you on the same page?

Sometimes people who were abused by their parents stay victims all of their lives, or they become abusers to their own families. Others are greatly repelled by violence and are wonderful with their children.

Smothering Relationships

These are exhausting. You are accountable all the time. You cannot go out without lots of phone calls to check on you or to say things like, "I need you," "I am not well," or "the children are sick and missing you."

Your health is fussed over, and if you don't look well, you are restricted from going out and having fun. You can be convinced that you are not well enough to go out with your friends or that your partner is not well and you can't possibly leave them alone.

This is another method of control, where your partner has a huge lack of confidence and has to be with you nearly all the time—creating the need to smother.

People like this will watch the clock and find a reason to stand between you and a member of the opposite sex. They find many reasons why you should not go out alone, and if you do, they put on a huge performance. If you dress up and look lovely, you are accused of looking for another partner, as you really do not need to dress up for other people. They completely and deliberately miss the fact that you have dressed up out of a sense of pride in yourself.

Abusers are generally rude to your friends and family, making it too uncomfortable for them to visit you. The flip side is that abusers may be utterly charming when your family is with you and may act like you are the most precious person in the world—and then they act spitefully or violently toward you when the visitors go home.

Excessive Need for Attention

When you are in a conversation with others, abusers will butt in to get your attention. They need continual praise, and you may find that you have to compliment them in front of others to keep them feeling secure. They will continually touch and claim you in a way different from the loving affection of a secure partner. They find it difficult to accept that you have friends of the opposite sex.

Tantrums on Arriving Home

If your controller feels they have lost control during time out, be prepared for some mind-blowing ranting and raving when their jealousy explodes. They will accuse you of flirting—or being flirted with and doing nothing to stop it. You may be completely bemused by what is happening. It's as if you are each viewing a different evening. My suggestion here would be to call the abusers bluff. Tell them you are sorry you make them so unhappy and that you are very willing to move on from the relationship so they can find someone who they would be better suited to.

Abusers may feel the need to tell lies about the people around you so you will stop seeing them. They need to make your decisions for you—just to help out—and to claim you by continually touching you inappropriately when you are out in mixed company or by commenting on your skills in the bedroom.

In readings, I am sometimes shown that person being thrown against walls, kicked, punched, urinated on, shaken, and screamed at. I feel their terror and have no hesitation in repeating what I am seeing, as I know that the information is only given to me by my guides if it is time to help the person make a positive change.

If you are experiencing these problems, there are many trained counsellors out there to go to for help, or you might like to try a spiritual reader/healer who works with the issues withheld in the chakras.

Withholding Sex

This rarely works. A person might get five minutes of attention or pleading, but it is the beginning of many future problems. Your sex life is for the pleasure of both partners. Try to keep it out of emotional conflicts, using communication skills to make a point. If you genuinely cannot forgive your partner, set yourself free to start again. Withholding sex or love will only lead to further separation at an emotional level.

If you are withholding sex after your partner has had sex with someone else, explain that you need time to process and that you expect understanding. However, it doesn't take years to forgive someone.

Being Put into Prostitution by a Lover or Husband

Unfortunately this happens when the finances are low, and some men will take this option. If it is with the woman's approval, then it is none of the reader's business. If, however, the woman complies because she fears the outcome of not doing what she's told, you may be able to help.

Let me share a particular case. I did a tarot reading for a newly married young lady. The girl was married to a station hand and was living in the beautiful outback.

I saw so many problems in front of her, although at that particular time everything was okay with her marriage. I could see her and her husband moving to the nearest capital city, taking her far from her family, and I felt the strong presence of drugs and prostitution. I felt that she would be involved against her will and that life would be horrible for her. I saw verbal and physical abuse and much unhappiness heading her way.

As I was telling her this, she was very annoyed with me, but I felt very strongly that this was accurate information. I suggested to her that at her worst moment—which would be in hospital after being bashed—she should phone her mother to come and get her, and her mother would be instrumental in saving her life. She left me a very cross girl, not believing a word of my reading. Over two years later, this girl and her mother visited me to thank me. Everything had turned out as I had predicted, and her mother did go and get her. She was finally clear of danger, and her life was back on track.

Withholding Forgiveness

This involves letting your partner pay again and again for a slight betrayal.

If you decide to forgive a person, just do it with all of your heart. Forgiveness is the journey of the older soul. Those who cannot forgive have many similar lessons in front of them, until they find that special place in their hearts to forgive unconditionally. You are not expected to forget what happened but only to learn from the experience. Maybe that person came to earth especially to open your heart to forgiveness. We do not know the bigger picture. Holding on to bitterness and resentment is a road to health problems.

Verbal Abuse in Public and at Home

Speaking rudely to your partner or embarrassing them in public with your side of the story will spell the end of a relationship. Speaking to the person you love most on earth should be a joyful experience. Love and light shine in your voice, and a person can feel the love you send every time you speak to them.

Verbal abuse is shattering. The energy of your aura shrinks from the onslaught of harsh, negative comments. Being shouted at is very unnerving, especially if this hasn't been part of your earlier life. It is distressing to think that the other person has lost control in this embarrassing way, and it shatters the equilibrium of your own energy field. No one has the right to shout at you.

When you are put down by the comments of others, your self-esteem is affected and your confidence ebbs, or you find yourself shouting back and losing control of yourself, which is something that you will later regret.

No one can tell you how to think or feel. These emotions belong to you, and it doesn't matter what other people think of you. They probably have their own reasoning based on their own lack of self-esteem. It really matters that you love and approve of yourself, that you do your best in every situation to act with dignity and honesty. If you find yourself feeling scared, ask your spirit guide to draw close to you for help and support. Sometimes the words that come out of your mouth do not go through your head first; they are the words of spirit.

If you find yourself in a situation where, every day of your life, you are in the wrong, continually being corrected or being made to feel inadequate, use your positive affirmations. Take a stand and refuse to be treated in that way, and maybe consider whether this is how you want to live the rest of your life. The well-known comment that "we teach people how to treat us" is very true. Know your own value and be true to yourself. Help is always at hand if you need it.

Problems a Reader May Have to Cope With

Dealing with Angry People at a Reading

It is embarrassing to watch people lose control of their emotions, unable to control their anger, and enter into a state of rage and confusion.

When people lose their tempers, the blood rushes to their extremities, making them want to punch or kick something or someone. This often leaves them incapable of clarity and sound reasoning.

Use a soft voice. Do not try to out-yell them. Let them talk, and when there is a gap, ask if you can now have your say. If they are not ready to listen, then you can listen some more and try again a little later.

If you tell an angry person that you are embarrassed for them because they have lost control, they may slow down. You can also suggest that they take a walk and then come back.

Why do people lose control of their tempers in a reading? It is simply because you have not said in the reading what they wanted to hear. Fortunately this is rare.

Dealing with People Who Live with an Angry Person

Some people live in fear. When anger is directed at them, they cringe, filling their cells with fear, hopelessness, and terror.

Anger and abuse may be family traits or learned behaviour, but they can be changed if the person wants to change them.

If no effort is made to change this destructive behaviour, then the partner may need to move on for personal safety or for the safety of any children.

Dealing With People Who Can't Control Their Anger

Many people who are angry cannot express themselves properly, so they yell, dominate conversations, need to always be right, sulk for days, punch holes in the walls, and in general upset themselves and everyone around them.

Encourage these people to get counselling and to go to stress management and anger management classes to learn how to change anger into assertiveness.

Too Much Interference from Family Members

Suggest that your client might like to sit down with the offending person or persons and explain that they (the client) want the opportunity to make their own decisions and mistakes and that they will be happy to ask for help if needed.

Teach clients to say no—or to find phrases that mean no, if they are not able to say the word. Suggestions include: "Thank you for your ideas. I will consider them"; "It is not appropriate for me at this time"; "I would prefer not to"; "I am busy on that day, as I have some things to do for myself"; or "I will get back to you if I am free at that time."

An answering machine can screen all calls. This allows people to refrain from answering or to think about an answer before being put on the spot. They might even ask their partners to deal with the problem occasionally.

See less of the people who interfere, go out more, avoid being so available, or tell people you need more personal space.

People Who Constantly Break Promises to Themselves or Others

Explain to people that every promise they break is like throwing a brick into their solar plexus chakra. It is a lump of negativity that must be removed, or it will affect the flow of the chakra, causing ill health in this area of the body.

Talk to the person about the value of self-talk and the importance of being positive in their thoughts, words, and actions. Ask them to look at promises as sacred vows to themselves and to others. Impress upon them the importance of being true to their word. Point out that mature people are capable of keeping their promises, whereas younger souls may struggle.

Personal Boundaries for the Reader

"Live by example" is a good motto for readers. Be punctual, be well-dressed, have clean hands and nails, and look your best. This will inspire confidence and encourage your clients to maintain a level of respect.

Try to stay within the allotted time for your readings so you don't get behind for the day and have people waiting around and getting annoyed.

Reading for People Who Are Unable to Form Boundaries

Encourage these people to love and respect themselves, to know that they are worthwhile and wonderful people. Teach them that everything that happens in life is a lesson and that they should look at it that way. This will give them the strength to want to pass each lesson. Discuss with them the areas where they have trouble holding their personal boundaries, and give some sound advice to help them.

Equality

The rules of equality shift according to the beliefs of the people in a relationship. Their beliefs will be based on childhood beliefs and the way they saw their parents interact with each other.

Spirit told me that the man is usually the protector and the woman is usually the nurturer. One person is not better than the other; they are just two halves put together to provide safety and compassion in a relationship or in a family. Some of us seem to share both of these traits, so the positions may be reversed.

Topics like division of housework, discipline of children, and finances should be thoroughly discussed before the wedding so that both partners know where they stand. Marrying a lazy person is a disappointment. However, it is your choice to stay and make positive changes or to move on.

Open discussion with good listening skills can solve most problems.

The Silent Treatment

People in relationships often have to deal with the silent treatment, where one partner does not have good communication skills or gets what they want by acting like a spoilt child. Sulking is childish behaviour, and this person cannot confront the problem and sort it out with maturity. This is common behaviour for people who do not get their own way—or when their partner gives someone else more attention than they themselves are getting.

Parents are known to do this to their children—if the children fail to agree with them, come home late, or make friends they do not approve of. The silent treatment is designed to make a person feel ashamed or guilty, as if they are the greatest disappointment in the other person's life.

If sulking works for us as children—getting us attention or our own way—we will continue it into adulthood.

Violence

Some people live in total fear of their partners, parents, grandparents, or siblings. Beatings are unfortunately part of some people's lives; the recipients are destroyed mentally and emotionally and hurt physically. Being hit with coat hangers or straps, burnt by cigarettes, or urinated on, some people have very sad lives. They may feel helpless and too ashamed to ask for help. You may see some of this behaviour when you are reading. Address it and see if you can help. In my experience, it usually takes several months before such a person comes back to me, ready for practical help to move on. Always recommend counselling.

Control Over Children

Here are some examples of control in a family: The other siblings can go out, but you have to stay home. Other children can play until six o'clock, but you have to be inside by four thirty. If you go out for an evening, you are the one who has to leave early and be home long before your friends. You are not be allowed to go out with your friends, as they are perceived as a bad influence on you. You have lots of chores that prevent you from going out during the week, and maybe you have to do the washing and ironing on the weekends while your siblings are out playing. In such cases, it may be impossible for a child to live up to a parent's expectations.

Here is a case in point. My friend was brought up in England on a farm. She loved the area, and as a child she was someone who tried hard to please. However, her mother was extremely manipulative and controlling. My friend's every day was controlled: she wasn't allowed to play with the other children until dark, and she was always called inside early, where she could hear the other children playing without her.

Beatings were part of her life, her father being tough on both her and his wife. He had the power over everyone, and her mother had the power over her two daughters. It was an extremely difficult family to be part of. Bullying, sulking, and beatings were all part of her upbringing.

When she met her husband, she went into a relationship where the man again held the power, and she tried hard to please him. He also hit her and made her life miserable. There were issues between her husband and her mother, and she was expected to make the peace at any price. This taught her to be manipulative, copying the energy of her mother.

She was strict with her own children and didn't see what she was doing until many years later, when she found herself on the phone talking to a friend. During their conversation, she complained about her children and realized that she was using the same words her mother had used. In fact, she had become just like her mother. She was a bully to her children and a coward with her controlling husband. She realized how unhappy her mother had made her, and from that moment on, she started to create changes in her thinking and actions. Her relationship with her children has greatly improved and continues to do so.

This lovely lady now works as a healer and counsellor. She is single and is enjoying her life and her freedom.

Before Getting Married

You can suggest to young people that they have a big think about how the parents of their potential partner deal with their own issues. These people are your partner's role models. If one person is a controller, manipulator, or alcoholic, or has a violent temper or beats the children, warning bells should be going off. Can the partner be very different? Yes, they can, but take notice of how they handle stress and whether they have good manners and speak well to others. If they come from a loving home, this bodes well for the future, but always be observant. Many people become so wrapped up with the wedding that they do not look very far beyond their special day.

Relationship Problems

Lack of love, lack of attention, and lack of appreciation are key factors in a relationship breaking down.

We all need praise. We all need attention to help make us feel special in the eyes of someone we love. Self-love comes first, but we need the lovely energies that connect us to our partner. Affection is very important: a touch, smile, wink, kind word, hug, bunch of flowers, gifts, unexpected dinners, and weekends away.

Saying thank you is also very important. Over the years we tend to just get on with it as our jobs become mundane, and we forget to say those little but important words. It is easy to lose your self-worth in a relationship where there is no praise or thanks.

Appreciation is the glue that keeps us feeling good about the things we do and say to our partner. We all need to feel that we are doing a good job and that our attention and the little things we do are appreciated. If you remember that love, appreciation, and showing affection is very important, so will your partner, and you will have a more loving relationship.

Jealousy

Jealousy comes from feeling inadequate. You are not jealous of someone unless you feel that they have something you do not have. Learning from someone you are jealous of is easier than letting the jealousy eat at you, making you and your partner very unhappy. Many people fight this negative trait and defeat it with maturity when they learn that they are very special in their own right.

We each have our own talents and skills to bring into the world and our relationships. Our partners are attracted to us and choose to be with us because of who we are.

If our partners choose to move on, it might not be because of anything we do or say. It could simply be that the time is right for change. They may have made the choice—before they came to earth—to move on and marry more than once. We can't hold someone to our side with dogged willpower. We can simply love and appreciate them, and the future will come out as it is meant to be.

CHAPTER 10

Reading for Friends and Family

I t is often difficult to read for the people you love. I think there are times when it is better for those closest to you to go to another reader. If, however, you do decide to read for friends and family—and yes, I do at times—ask for help and be open to whatever comes up.

At some time you may have someone in your family with a terminal illness, as I did with my father who had brain cancer. My cards showed his death from October, long before he was diagnosed or, in fact, had any symptoms. He passed over in February the following year. I did not pass this information on to him. There are times when you really do not want to know these things, so be careful when reading for family members. If you have one or more people with terminal illness or serious sickness, the answers may be in their readings instead of yours.

The flip side of this is that you may have access to warnings of ill health and be able to help the person by sending them to the doctor, doing complimentary healing on them, helping them to alter any negative thought patterns, and giving hope, strength, and encouragement. Many people have a better quality of life because of their positive attitudes and willingness to embrace all ideas—from doctors, specialists, healers, and natural therapies.

I have seen this in action with my husband, who has cardiomyopathy, and my brother-in-law, who had cancer. These two strong men have done everything in their power to have not only a life, but a very good and loving life, and I am proud of their endeavours and the example they have set for others. They have both been in a position to give help and encouragement to others with health problems.

Sometimes an illness is just a warning to change our way of life or our way of thinking. If we can work our way through these changes, healing is helped. If we are heading down a very negative pathway, we can make huge changes to our lives.

Can all of us save our own lives? Maybe, sometimes. It depends on our karma and the decisions we have made in spirit. However, it is always worth putting one hundred percent into trying, being open to challenge and change, and really wanting your life with a passion.

My sister-in-law refers to dying as "catching the bus." Maybe sometimes we have to catch the bus to our spiritual home so we will be ready for the return journey and the next set of lessons—or to be a guide for our grandchildren or family members. One thing is for sure: one day we will all catch that bus.

Positive affirmations are an excellent way to improve our lives. We can say them anywhere: in the car, when we are out walking, in bed, doing dishes, going to work. They do not take up a lot of the day, but they serve to remind us that we create our own destinies and that we can improve our lives day by day.

It is comforting to sit and meditate and ask for pure, white light from the universe to shine on us or onto someone we love who needs healing. I work a lot with the reiki energy for healing and also with the white light or golden-white Mahatma energy. Good results also come from coloured healing and symbols. Ask spirit to help you in your endeavours for even better results. Blue or green energy brings down high blood pressure; yellow energy dries up mucus and helps you to study. Red warms our bodies, so it is a good colour to wear in winter. Blue eases and cools you if you have a fever, and violet helps to ease a bad headache or migraine. Colour plays an important role in all of our lives.

CHAPTER 11

How Psychic Are You?

How psychic are you?

Do you have gut feelings, instincts, and hunches?

We all have these feelings from time to time, but we don't always pay attention to them. How often have you exclaimed, "I knew that!" after the event?

Women often say they know something intuitively. Men mention the "gut feelings" that they have in business and at home. Business people have strong intuition or gut feelings. This makes the difference between average business returns and an excellent business that is moving forward into huge profits.

Do you know when your children are lying to you? Most parents have a good "it-is-not-so" barometer.

Are you aware when someone is about to visit to surprise you? How often are you thinking about someone, and then they knock on the door? Do you suddenly just know what is in the letter you have just received? You can have very strong feelings about what is in a letter or who it is from. If it is a bill, maybe you can tell the amount. Can everyone do this? No. Only some people have this skill. We often have different skills from those around us. We can, however, build on the skills that we have.

Do you know when to phone a friend because you feel that they are distressed? Do you hear the phone ring and hurry to it, as you are suddenly lifted with happy energy? Can you see in your mind's eye where the person is ringing from? Do you sometimes wake up in the morning knowing where to find a missing article?

Ask for this information before you go to sleep at night, and there will be times when you will wake up and just know.

You can also ask to have things returned to you. My brother gave me a lovely set of sapphire earrings and pendant. I misplaced them when we moved and thought them to be lost. Thinking about them about a year later, I asked spirit if they could find them for me, and then I forgot all about them. One morning I went into the bathroom, and there I saw a folded, clean, white tissue. Inside I found my missing and very dirty jewellery. I could hardly believe my eyes, and I am very grateful for their return. Over the years, my family has seen the return of books, articles of clothing, and an icing sifter. No, it isn't always something exciting, only very useful.

If you ask spirit a question, sometimes the answer will just pop into your head during the day. It is always worth asking. Often the answer will come when you are daydreaming, cleaning, or resting. I asked spirit once why I couldn't get my answers straightaway. The reply was, "We need you to get out of the way, stop searching for the answer, and just be. Then we can get through to you." So, ask your question and be patient in waiting for your answer.

Do you walk past a photograph of someone you love who has passed over and say hello? Can you feel the answer? Can you feel the love? Spirit people will always hear you and answer you. They are always thrilled when you acknowledge them. They can see you clearly, hear you clearly, and speak to you. The veil between dimensions is thinning. As we all raise our vibrations, we will connect in a deeper way to other dimensions where our loved ones reside.

These feelings all come from your intuition, which is steadily sending out signals for you to receive and process. We are awakening and starting to understand that there is no death, only a transition to another place. We are becoming open to meditation and to listening for spiritual answers to problems. We are opening our minds to the possibility of other dimensions and planes of existence. We understand that it is possible for other people to live in other galaxies. Maybe they do not live like us or look like us, but we are being conditioned to this fact by the number of diverse people and cultures we interact with on earth.

We live in the third dimension. There are other planes of existence in this dimension, as there are in other dimensions. Have you heard of other aspects of yourself living parallel lives to yours at this time? Some of your aspects live on earth, and some live on other planes of existence. The universe is huge. We are a tiny planet in the big picture, a planet designed for us to live on and learn about duality and separation from the source. Some of us will find the answers more quickly than others. It is a tougher journey for people who are very left-brained, who are often sceptical and rude about people who are right-brained. Left-brained people work with logic, routine, discipline and facts and need everything to be proven. Try to be open in your thoughts and accept the fact that not everyone sees the world as you do, and all realities are valid.

Many right-brained people work with colours and unexplained ideas and realities, and they have a total belief in spirit and are usually creative and artistic. It is our challenge to let go of judgment of others and to find our own way through the mysteries.

All artistic endeavours link us to spirit and to the creative world. Music takes us to a different reality in our minds, as do lovely pictures, excellent photography, and books filled with scenic landscapes. All forms of sculpture soothe our souls and bring us pleasure. Meditation is one of our greatest methods of connecting to our personal spirit guides.

Third Eye

Have you ever closed your eyes and seen an eye in front of you? Sometimes the eye is open, and sometimes it is closed. There will be times when it opens before you and you see the iris. You are looking at your own third eye. You might like to talk to it and give it some exercises to do—for example, to look left or right, blink, open, or close. You will gradually build a rapport with this stunning feature.

Love and Blessings

I send out love and blessings to my friends and family by name every night before I go to sleep. I include in this list my loved ones who have passed over and my spirit teachers. No matter which side of the veil they reside on, they are very special to me.

I send out healing energy, forgiveness, symbols, white light, positive affirmations, and best wishes to a lot of people, including healing energy to mother earth and to trouble spots around the world. I ask forgiveness if I have hurt anyone, and I try to change my attitude if I feel it has been lacking in any area. What do you say in your prayers? Hopefully, I have given you some suggestions.

You can send out love and blessings any time of the day. You can add these good wishes to your positive affirmations when you are a passenger in a car or when you are having your daily walk.

Students

Serious students will spend some time nearly every day working on raising their intuitive abilities with mind exercises. It is an exciting challenge, one you are up for if you are reading this book. Go for it. Use the exercises in this book on a regular basis, and you will fly with the eagles. Your colours will brighten, and you will feel the love and the energy pouring into your body.

Can you miss a day? Of course you can. I don't work at night if I have had an alcoholic drink. I show my spirit teachers respect, and I suspect they really don't want to listen to me giggling and being totally irreverent.

Sometimes you will be out late and won't feel like working when you come home. Sometimes you may just be too tired. We are living in physical bodies that slow us down, wear out, and need a rest after a hard day. Don't be hard on yourself. Just make a commitment to work several nights a week and do the very best you can. You will notice a steady improvement. If you are a morning person, set a time to work in the early hours when everything is quiet.

Mantras

Working with mantras will improve your concentration and focus. Try one-word mantras like *love*, *harmony*, or *peace*, and say them over and over, stilling your mind and finding that special, quiet place.

I like to work with the word *peace*. I say it and see it, over and over, holding my focus for as long as I can. If I lose focus, I simply open my eyes, close them, and start again. Concentration is very important in your work. Take the time to work on your mantras.

You can also use a phrase as a mantra. Some suggestions might be: *May I live in peace* or *I accept peace and love into my heart*. Work out the phrase that means the most to you, and work with it several times a week, sitting quietly and just working your mantra. Affirmations can also be used as mantras, and there are many lovely ones for you to choose from.

Chakra Clearing

It is a really good idea to sit down on a regular basis and run some energy into your chakra system. It will help to purify and revitalize your energetic system. Here is an exercise for you to try.

Sit quietly or lie down. Close your eyes. Imagine a pure-white light shining onto your red-base chakra, which looks a little dull. As the light shines, the chakra brightens. Ask to release any problems from this chakra into the light. You are giving yourself the opportunity to forgive anyone in your family who has hurt you or to forgive yourself if you have hurt anyone accidentally or on purpose. Ask for the energy and vitality to live your life to the fullest. Visualize your chakra becoming a lovely, clear red and your mind exercise being successful.

Move the light to the sacral chakra, and see that your chakra is a murky orange. As the pure-white light shines on your chakra, let go of a jealousy issue. Work out who you are jealous of and simply let it go. Know that this is being caused by your own lack of confidence, and think of something you can do to build your confidence. See the problem dissolving, as your chakra turns into a rich and lovely shade of orange. Ask for the creative ideas that will lead you into a better place in your life. Ask for this clear, rich, orange chakra to give you inspiration and enhanced creativity.

Move your consciousness and the white light to the solar plexus chakra, and notice that this chakra is a muddy yellow. Let the light shine in, and as it does, work out where you need to work with honesty. Gossip doesn't work. You only *think* other people don't know of your gossip. The only person you are fooling is yourself. Let go of your need to gossip, your need to feel important by having more information than others for your three minutes of fame. The light is clearing this negativity out of your system, so rejoice as you see your brilliant, yellow, healthy chakra.

Move the light to your heart chakra, and let the light shine. Let the green become rich and vibrant. Let this chakra know that you would welcome a deep and equal love into your life, that you would welcome someone you could love and who would love you. Ask to be filled with compassion and empathy, kindness and understanding. The green will brighten, and you will feel refreshed.

Now the light moves to the throat chakra, breaking up the darker blue and letting the light shine in. Ask for help with your communication problems, for help in speaking your truth with clarity and compassion. Let go of the boundaries that hold you back. You might like to ask for help with public speaking, writing a book, or taking classes. Ask for clarity and the right words to use for every occasion. The chakra is a now a lovely shade of azure blue.

You will move the light now to the brow chakra, illuminating the indigo and clearing any blockages that hold back your intuition. Ask for pictures, thoughts, and ideas to help yourself on your journey through life. Offer to always work with integrity and for the betterment of mankind.

Moving now to the crown chakra and infusing the white light with even more white light, ask to be connected to your sprit guides, angels, and spiritual teachers. Send love and blessings to those who need help, and give thanks for the good people or things in your life.

Ask for your chakra system to be balanced and open to new ideas and support from your inner guidance.

Grounding

To stay grounded while you work, you may like to walk outside on the lawn among the trees, breathing in the earth energy before you do readings. The earth energies are calming and stable, and they help you to concentrate and give sound advice.

Every plant sends out healing energy. It is its gift to you, so take it all on board and use it well. Pick up your own energy, and feel at peace. Some deep breathing in a garden is always a bonus. If you aren't working, you may just like to enjoy this peaceful time among the plants and elementals. It will also help to clear headaches and give you clarity.

If you have time, walk in a garden between appointments with clients, as this will refresh you so you are ready to work again. Our garden has some lovely, big crystals from Brazil that lift our energies. It is always a lovely place to recharge our batteries and to enjoy with our friends.

Advice from Spirit

Many years ago, as a young reader, I felt the need to tell people whatever they wanted to know when I was in their company. So many people have great fun asking silly things, like "What colour is my underwear?" or "Will I win lotto?"

Going out to dinner became unpleasant, as I would be bombarded by the cynic at the table and asked many questions. Even giving good answers is not enough if the person is not enlightened. The barrage of questions only continues, as people like this do not take time to reflect and think about the answers you are giving. If they are still playing in the lower energies, my answers would never be enough. My answers are not based on logic, only on what *is*.

I work with trust, faith, honesty, and the help of my intuition and my spirit helpers. I don't think that I am better than anyone else. In fact, there are readers and mediums on earth that I greatly admire, and my training continues daily and will do so forever.

One day my guide came to me and told me to never feel the need to prove myself. He said that those who believed in spirit would accept whatever I gave them, even if it was nothing of great importance. Those who didn't believe, never would believe, so I would be tested over and over again if I played their games. He told me to walk my own path and not be influenced by the criticism or doubts of others, as they would come to their own understanding when the time was right. I took his advice to heart and no longer feel the need to do parlour tricks to impress people. I hope these words of wisdom from spirit will help you as well.

Brazil

It was interesting to find a statue outside of John of God's Healing Center in Brazil that carried these lines: "For those who believe, anything is possible. For those who do not believe, there is no possible answer." I have found those words to be very true.

Respect

As a reader you need to have strong boundaries, otherwise you will live your life in a state of exhaustion and will not have time for your own family and friends. If you are a reader, it is your vocation, not something you do for fun in a pub or to make yourself popular. Respect yourself, be professional, and help to give our career a good name.

Respect the guides who come in to work with you. Does it all have to be serious? No, it does not. I have a lot of laughs with my guides. They always speak well to me and encourage me to keep trying and to always do the best I can. However, I take the information seriously and relay it as it is given to me. I find that if I change things to soften them or to be kind, I miss something fundamental in the exchange. So now I just trust and repeat information as it is given to me.

Integrity

Integrity is so important for a reader. You will not always have the answer a person seeks, so always be honest. I only take a person's first name and phone number. If anything comes up after they have left, I can get in touch. This rarely happens, but it is better to have the phone number. I don't need surnames and prefer not to know.

Empathy

You will at times be very touched by a reading and may choose to do some reiki on your client before they leave in order to balance them. You may not agree with how they live their lives, but it's not for you to judge, as you do not know how you would behave in their position, or what choices they made in spirit before coming to earth.

I have read for people from many different walks of life —including prostitutes, whom I have found to be delightful ladies doing a job I couldn't do. I have read for people who have committed crimes and who are trying to make a new life. I have done readings for hard-nosed businessmen who spend their lives being sharks in a pool, all vying for the top jobs and often feeling empty in their hearts. They cope with pressure and stress that I know nothing about, and I hope they will take the time to smell the roses. All the people I read for are special to me. They give me their trust, and in return I give them advice to consider, and comfort from spirit.

We are all in this together, all the people of earth. No matter what our jobs, we are all trying to find our way through the mazes that life presents to us. Let's help each other and, at all times, be kind and respectful of others. I ache for those who do not love or are not loved on earth, but I know in my heart that they are dearly loved by spirit and are never really alone.

When you commit to a reading, you are giving love and support to the person with you. You are passing on information from spirit without judgment and with empathy and compassion. It is a lovely job and one to be taken seriously.

It doesn't matter whether you go on to read only for yourself or for others. It is a way of opening your channel to spirit and to higher learning. Enjoy every step of the journey and your connection to your own spirit guide.

Chapter 12

Questions about Spirit and Our Guides

What is *clairvoyance*?

The word *clairvoyance* refers to "clear seeing" or having clear visions. This happens when you receive clear pictures from the spirit world to assist you with your readings. You will see with your mind's eye events that you are not taking part in, events with people you may or may not recognize. Usually, you will not be given a time frame, but do note the ages of the participating people or the mode of dress. These facts may be of assistance to you. Your focus shifts slightly (mine to the right), so you are conscious of both worlds but paying attention to spirit world and their messages.

What is *clairaudience*?

Clairaudience refers to "clear hearing," the ability to hear spirit on a subtle level. At times there will be a ringing in your ears—or static, like tuning in to a radio station. You may, in the early stages of clairaudience, lie in bed listening to two people in the spirit world chatting very softly, so softly that you can hear the voices but not understand the words. At any time of the day or night, you may hear spirit call out your name. They are looking to make a connection with you.

What is *clairsentience*?

Clairsentience refers to "clear feelings." If you are clairsentient, you may feel the emotions radiating from other people—emotional pain, guilt, and loneliness.

What do clairvoyants mean when they speak about *knowing*?

Sometimes we just know something. It comes from a deep inner knowing and is always right. This information is just in your head, and you have no doubt that it is correct. My guide refers to *knowing* as the highest skill.

What is an *empath*?

An *empath* is someone who will often put the needs of others before their own. Empaths are kind, compassionate, and very caring. They are noted for their serenity and sensitivity toward others and toward animals. They may be sensitive to loud noise and prefer not to be in airports or busy shopping centres or with very loud people. They may also be light-sensitive. They are highly intuitive, drawing many people to them for help and understanding. Cruelty makes them physically sick or tearful. They can be extremely upset by news of earthquakes, flooding, and brushfires, as they feel the pain and emotions of those involved in the disaster.

Can you explain *spiritual counselling*?

Spiritual counsellors work in many different ways. Their skills come from reading the aura and working through issues associated with the chakra system and past-life therapy. If they are mediums, they can bring solace to the client with validated information from their loved ones.

Can I change the date that I am supposed to die?

I believe we often have more than one exit point from this earth. It depends on what pathways we follow. If we have completed our tasks early, we can leave early or go ahead with another set of lessons. If we have missed important lessons, they can be "re-presented" if our lives are extended. I believe this is all worked out in spirit before we come to earth.

Sometimes we may stay so that someone can save our lives—or so that we can save or assist someone else, negating some of our karma.

Most people believe there is only one exit point, but this will be something for you to decide.

Does my guide watch me in the shower or toilet?

Guides would not watch you in the shower; they would respect your privacy. As I am a short, fat lady, I suspect my guides would fall out of heaven laughing at even a peek!

Do my guides get mad at me? Do they leave me if I am naughty or bad?

Your guides are your friends and teachers. They may be disappointed with your decisions at times, but they recognize that it is your right to have free will on earth and to make any decision you want. No, they do not leave you. Many of these guides have walked the earth walk and have made the same mistakes you may be making. This is part of the learning experience. They are patient, kind, and sincere, and they love you very much. We do not give up on our children when they make mistakes; we simply help them. We are proud of them when they succeed, and we honour them when we see evidence of kindness and integrity. It is the same with our spirit guides.

We are human, so it is okay to make mistakes. Sometimes our greatest lessons come to us this way.

Do we know if we are making a wrong choice?

I believe we usually know when we are making a wrong choice. Morally, we know. Spirit says, "If you have to hide what you are doing, then maybe you shouldn't be doing it." Think your actions through properly. Breaking into someone's house or car, or sleeping with the boss to get a promotion, are examples of wrong choices. If you are ashamed of your behaviour, if you know you are going to hurt someone by your actions, make positive changes.

Sometimes we are simply wilful and will not listen to anyone. At that time in our journey, we may find it necessary to put down others who try to help us, to be stubborn to the point of our own detriment, and to insist on always being right. We may never see that there are often many answers to the same problem and that the one we have chosen could be improved. Wilfulness, loneliness, and emptiness often go hand-in-hand with wrong choices. Give yourself every opportunity for success. Your guides may well have bought your helpers into your life for a good reason, but they may not be able to get through to you.

If you are having a hidden affair, remember the law of karma: what you do to others will return to you, if not in this lifetime, then in another. Also bear in mind that over 69 percent of second marriages do not last. Ask yourself if you are repeating the lessons you failed to learn in your first marriage, and look for the similarities—or you may be moving on to another set of lessons.

Through all of our troubles and experiences, our guides love us and try to protect us. Remember that some of these experiences are ones that we have set up for ourselves, so our guides will not judge us or drop us. They will step closer to our sides with love.

Is everyone good enough to have a guide?

Yes. We all come to earth as a blank page, with the story of our lives yet to write. Our guides show compassion and helpfulness. They wish us well and do not judge us. They simply go right on helping us with good suggestions and good contacts who can help us, and they send us to the right people—doctors, readers, and friends—when we need them. Guidance is worked out in spirit before we incarnate, and our guides will never let us down. I know that they are always there, loving and supporting us.

Do handicapped children have guides?

Yes, they certainly do. Usually their guides are older souls who support them well and will also watch over the mother and father to see if *they* can help the child to grow as much as possible. The souls of handicapped children come from two different groups. Some are very old souls who are here to learn humility and to teach the parents compassion and responsibility. Kindness shows in their eyes, and they are learning to be completely dependent on others. I am sure you will agree that that is a very difficult road to choose. These souls are usually very loving. They like to be cuddled, and they bring warmth and joy into the home. It is a very humbling experience to have to be totally dependent on another person.

Other souls who take the journey of a handicapped child may be damaged souls who need a lot of love and attention to help them back onto their pathway.

The parents of these children are special. They are trusted to look after these children twenty-four hours a day, seven days a week—usually with very little respite. Some of these "handicapped" souls are violent, spiteful, and difficult to handle. It is interesting to see how many fathers bolt from this situation, leaving young mums to battle on alone. Lack of responsibility is a big thing when you have a handicapped child. Even if both parents are not living together, spirit would hope that the caring is shared by both parents and that the main caregiver has adequate holidays, as he or she lives a life of exhaustion. Spirit gives full credit to parents who both stay and do the very best they can—hopefully, with family and government help. They have taken on a very important task, and they are kind and caring souls who are doing a wonderful job.

Are we all at the same stage of development?

We are definitely not all at the same stage of development. "Young souls" refers to those who are slow with their lessons. They need to repeat their lessons many times before they get them right and move on to the next set of lessons and the next set of guidance. Many angels help at this level, and they are also often sent to help children or troubled souls. For instance, a person may choose to be an alcoholic several lifetimes in a row before realizing they can cope perfectly well in this world without substance abuse. A young soul will go to many readers, friends, or family members for advice but probably will not take any of it on-board until ready. This can take days, weeks, or years.

Younger souls are much more selfish, and they value materialism, good looks, fame, and the limelight. They are often manipulative and controlling. Some are in abusive relationships through lack of self-esteem. They refuse to let go and to forgive, dragging these heavy energies with them through lifetime after lifetime.

"Older souls" learn quickly, and they may have had some of their lessons in other planes or dimensions. They help others as part of their training in patience, tolerance, and love. They are more compassionate and caring, and they are less likely to let people walk over their boundaries, as they have self-respect. They find it easy to forgive, and they understand the value of letting *love* be the answer. They have great respect for the elderly, the handicapped, and people who are suffering in third-world countries and for mother earth.

Whatever your level, you are here to learn, and everyone is equally important. I see the older souls as people who reach back on the pathway to give a hand to others who are struggling—and who reach forward to those who will give them a hand when it is their turn to struggle with their lessons. We are all of humanity, in this together, making our way into the light and into awareness.

Are our guides at the same stage of development?

No, they are not. Young souls require guides who can meet their needs, and their guides may have travelled down pathways similar to theirs on earth. Young souls do not have spiritual awareness; it is developed as they learn the lessons in their chakras and develop grace. Their problems relate to their ability to survive, the way they treat others, and what they think about themselves. There are many lesson to work through on earth, and some are much harder than others.

As you grow and start to awaken, some of your guides will change, and you will be given the best guide to help you through the next set of lessons. As you work from the heart chakra, the bad news is that it all gets harder; the lessons are tougher and more is expected of you. The good news is that it is fabulous: you learn and understand at a deeper level and are taking lessons on-board every day of your life. You strive to keep up: to show empathy, compassion, warmth, and caring, and to be balanced and sharing. You learn to give and to receive. You meet many wonderful people from all over the world who give you the opportunity to share your knowledge and to learn many new and wonderful things.

Guidance here is strong and very literal. Your guides come and go as you need them, and as you work, you are encouraged and taught at new levels. Then you have the opportunity to share your knowledge as a spiritual teacher, a caregiver, a healer, and so forth. Your guides from this level include spiritual masters, higher teachers, teachers from other planetary systems, and archangels.

Who is your spirit guide? Would you like to know how to get in contact with this very special person who is guiding you and helping you through this lifetime? You will have one special guide—and several others who will come in with specific jobs to do or lessons to teach you.

Your left brain likes to chatter to you as it finds the pictures from the right brain very boring. Keep your pictures or feelings flowing, and this will help to cut out the mindless chatter.

Meditation 1: Meet Your Spirit Guide

This meditation takes approximately fifteen minutes.

Close your eyes and envision walking through a beautiful rain forest. Smell the leaves under your feet and the sweet smell of the plants, and experience the shade of the protective trees.

See the vibrant, colourful flowers and enjoy their beauty. Which colours stand out in your mind? Smell the aromas of the forest, and see the dew on the leaves of the tall and magnificent trees.

Imagine small animals scurrying around your feet as they go about their day. Notice an animal on the side of the pathway or in the trees. Are there any birds in this beautiful place?

As you walk, you come to a set of four stone steps that rise up to an area out of your sight. They look very old and have been worn down with use.

Look at the four steps as you walk up them one step at a time—one, two, three, and pause—and then raise your hands out in front of you without looking up.

You will feel someone take your hands, and as you step up once more, look up. You will be looking into the eyes of your spirit guide.

Walk with your spirit guide in a lovely sacred garden, and find a seat to sit on while you chat. Ask for their name if they are not familiar to you. Ask your spirit guide to help you when you are learning how to do readings—or how to improve your readings if you are already a reader. Ask them which colour you should wear for a while to balance your energy bodies.

If you are feeling strong and have a good connection, ask as many questions as you like. If you are ready to leave, bid your spirit guide farewell and return to your room.

If you had trouble with this exercise, keep trying, using your imagination. Let your right brain have an opportunity to shut down the left side and work with you. Keep up the mind pictures if you are visual—or the feelings if you are not.

Questions to Answer and Record in Your Spiritual Journal

Which coloured flowers stood out for you? Can you relate the colours to your chakra system and see where you need healing? Do you know the name of your guide?

What message did your guide have for you? Can you describe your guide's appearance?

Which animals did you notice? Animals bring you messages. What did you learn from your animal? Remember their strengths: you may have them or need them. Did you see a bird? Was there a message from the bird? How wide was your pathway? How open are you to meditation and to the messages you will be given? Were you comfortable in this meditation? Was the path rough or smooth? How are you coping with your current lessons? How is your journey at the moment? What could you smell in the forest?

Which flowers, trees, or shrubs were in your sacred garden? When are you going to do this exercise again?

Record your meditation every time to see your growth.

Meditation 2: Connecting to Your Higher Self

This meditation takes approximately thirty minutes.

Close your eyes and relax. You may like to light candles and play soft, gentle music. Make sure you will not be disturbed for thirty minutes.

Feel yourself floating into wide-open spaces. Float now through clear, red energy and feel yourself lifting and feeling well and happy. Remind yourself of the security you have in your life, the family members and friends who support your journey, and the energy you have to achieve all of your dreams. Mention to yourself three dreams that you will manifest on earth.

Pause.

Now, float into orange energy and enjoy this feeling of creativity and fertility. See yourself painting a picture of the things you wish to create, such as: a future loving partner, children, a book, beautiful art, or yourself singing or dancing. Find the things that make your heart sing. Paint your face with a beautiful smile, filled with joy and happiness. Take some time to paint this picture.

Pause.

Now, float into a vibrant yellow. This colour fills you with self-confidence and self-esteem. Say to yourself: *I am a wonderful and loving person. I attract love into my life. I attract a loving partner. I am creating abundance on all levels. I am honest and reliable. I create my own destiny with love.*

Pause.

Now, float into a soft, green energy. This energy will balance you and make you feel at peace. In this energy I want you to see

71

the child you were at six years of age. Go to this child and give them a hug and tell the child that they are loved. Pause. Now go to the child you were at thirteen years of age and hug this child, telling them that you are proud of them and that you appreciate the efforts they have made on your behalf. Pause. Now go to the person you are today, and tell yourself how well you are doing. Give encouragement and sound advice to yourself.

Tell the universe that you are open to love.

Pause.

Float now into a sky-blue energy and think about the choices you have made in the last year. Is there anything you would like to change? Do you need a new job? Do you need to do a lot of repair work on your relationship? Do you need to move on in life? Are you ready for new challenges? Think about these things.

Pause.

Now float into indigo energy. You will feel that you are floating in a night sky, and you might like to add the sparkling stars. Think about the spiritual gifts you would like to have, and put them in order of preference. Would you like to see and read auras, read tarot, see clairvoyantly, be a medium, or do something else? Ask for whatever you would like to build on to help others.

Pause.

Now you will float even further to where the energy is pure-white. As you float, you will see ahead of you two chairs. On one chair sits your higher self. See your higher self step toward you and welcome you. Your higher self is responsible for all of your soul aspects. They oversee your earthly life and help whenever you ask for help. Your higher self knows your past lives and your probable future lives, all of which are ever changing as you develop.

Ask your higher self some questions.

Pause.

Ask your higher self for help in your readings.

Say good bye. Then float into a rainbow and back into your physical body, and be aware of the earth beneath you.

CHAPTER 13

How to Address Death in Readings

eath in a reading can refer to the end of a way of life and the beginning of another. The person you are reading for may be ready to make huge life changes, and you can encourage this.

I like to remind people that sometimes an event—like losing one's job—may seem like a complete disaster. But out of the disaster the sun will shine again, and they may find their way into a better job or another line of employment that fills their soul. It may even lead to new romance and many new friends. We need to learn to embrace death and call it rebirth, as much happiness may be waiting just around the corner for us.

In a card reading, I look for four to five cards in a row to tell me about physical death. It is never shown to me with only one card.

People have crossroads in their lives. Maybe a person has passed more tests than were originally planned, or maybe they have a life to save later. We will never know another person's entire journey. If we are given the opportunity to save a life in a reading, it must be treated with the utmost respect. It is my belief that we have more than one exit point from this planet—depending on how we are doing with our lessons, on whether we need to go "home" for a particular reason, or on how fast we are learning.

You can give the circumstances of an accident that may be prevented. You might give direction to a healer who may be of great service to a sick person. But remember that you can only pass on the information you are given. The outcome is still in the hands of the person you are reading for.

An example of this would be a client of mine. I had the pleasure of reading for his wife many years ago, and I saw his death, which was preventable. I asked her to send him to me for a reading before April of the following year. He put off seeing me until March when he finally turned up full of indignation and scepticism. I read for him, explaining what the cards meant and showing him the two different pathways ahead of him. One path would take him on a diving trip in April from which he would never return; the other took him onto the path of spirituality and healing, at which he would excel. I am happy to say that this man is now a business partner and firm friend of both my husband and myself. However, when he left me that day, I told my husband that I really didn't know if he was listening to me or not. My husband, who also has some great insights, replied that one day that man would be my best friend.

This is not a regular occurrence and has only happened to me a few times in this lifetime. I am always conscious of the karmic and emotional debt it carries.

I am also conscious that saving a life is not always meant to be. My brother drove away from me to his death in an accident when he was only twenty-two, and I was not given insight or warning that this was about to happen. Sometimes we just have to respect that it is time for the person to go home to spirit. I look at it as if they have gone on holiday and will be there when I arrive to reunite with them. I chat to my brother, knowing that the veil between worlds is very thin now and that he can receive every message I send to him. I send love and blessings to him and to other family members who have passed over.

There are no understandable reasons for the length of life a person will have or for whether a person will suffer with illness or be taken tragically in an accident. We do not know the karma of another person—or even our own karma. There is a much bigger plan, one that we cannot tap into at this stage of our learning. I believe that most illness comes from the chakra system breaking down or being overloaded.

I have been told by spirit that there is often more than one exit point for a person on earth. Depending on what they have achieved, what they came to do, and when they need to be home for their next exciting adventure to earth, the time line can change.

Predicting death is therefore not an easy thing to do. I believe I will only be told if it is necessary, and it will only happen on very rare occasions, when the person will greatly benefit from missing an accident.

I do not believe that we are privileged to know how many lives a person has on earth, as that information comes from the akashic records, which are only to be accessed by the relevant person seeking to find his or her own information, usually on return to the spirit world. I am sometimes told that a person has had a lot of lives. I am at times shown past lives that are relevant to the life being lived now.

Usually death in a reading refers to the end of a job, marriage, relationship, or way of life, and spirit provides new ideas for a fresh start for the person to consider. If my readings are ignored, I accept that this is the choice of the enquirer. My job is simply to supply information and choices and to make positive suggestions.

A reader does have to know when to turn off and move forward. If I feel upset or worried about something I have found in a reading, I will send love and blessing to the person in my nightly prayers and ask spirit to please love and protect them as they go on their journey. If I am dealing with a health issue, I will send healing energy to them to help them find balance.

Mediums read death and bring messages from the other side. Validating messages from loved ones helps enormously with the healing process. Mediums have a responsibility to be accurate and to show empathy and compassion in a reading. There are many great mediums available for private readings, and most of these hold regular shows throughout Australia and overseas.

CHAPTER 14

Types of Readings

We will be looking at many types of readings for you to work with and to enjoy. I find the readings fall into different categories.

The very basic psychic reading concerns career, ambition, home life, money, sport, envy, having children, and stressful lives. The client may also want to know about other people, so be very careful what you say. It is not their business or yours, so remember your tact and diplomacy.

The next category is about love and romance, successful partnership, marriage, improving communication skills, working with integrity, and diplomacy. This is a deeper reading. I find that when this type of reading happens, it is not my choice, and I am only guided by spirit.

The third category is health. I sometimes find myself looking into people's bodies where I see red spots of trouble, and I myself feel sick because they are very out-of-balance. From there come the questions that will help people change their lives and heal—if they choose to. People's emotions are fairly easy to see, and they are usually very stressed. This provides an opportunity to counsel them and send them to the appropriate help. Sometimes messages from their spiritual teachers come through—with sound help for them and encouragement for their futures. I have certificates in bereavement counselling and stress counselling in the workplace, and in anger management. I also have diplomas in professional stress consultancy, aromatherapy, and corporate stress management. These studies have given me greater insight into helping others.

The fourth category is mediumship, where you have the opportunity to pass on messages from loved ones who have left this planet. This requires tapping into spirit world, linking to a spirit person, and passing on the messages from the impressions you have been given. Many mediums are born with the ability to communicate with spirit from a young age; others train when the time is right to develop this talent.

I never know in advance what I am going to read for people. I clear my mind, call in my guides and the client's guides (if they choose to come), and only work when my client has arrived and they are ready to start. I like to work with a blank page, and for this reason the first reading I do for anyone is special for me. I know very good readers who like to gather information in advance, and that works very well for them, so I will leave it up to you which method suits you best. There isn't a right or wrong answer here.

There are many types of readings we will be working with—some of them discussed in this book. This book is designed to help beginners make a start and to help established readers add to their skills.

We will be working with flower readings (the beautiful flowers on earth are a joy to read), crystals, ribbons sticks, photographs, keys, cards, jewellery, artwork, overheads, and others.

As you learn to read, you will find you have favourites. Work through all of the exercises, as you never know which ones will resonate with you. For me, it is tarot cards, flower readings, overheads, and numerology. Being a medium gives greater depth to my readings and enables me to help people who are bereaved and who need help to heal. Enjoy your readings, and practice on friends and family until you are ready to start work in this field.

Enjoy building your skills and work always from the heart for the best results.

CHAPTER 15

Symbols

You will find that spirit people often send you symbols to interpret. It is up to you to work out what the various symbols mean to you. As I work with symbols in the healing field, I am often given symbols from reiki or Isis Seichim or any of the symbols I personally use for healing. I find these symbols are a huge help to me when I am doing a reading.

You may like to create a dictionary of symbols in your head for spirit to work with, instead of having to decode the symbol from spirit. They will be happy to work with yours, making your job a lot easier.

For example, when reading for a person, I may see a Sei He Ki from the reiki symbols. This would indicate to me that I needed to answer questions on how to access spirit guides, angels, and higher self. This person would be searching for a deeper reading, wishing to access their spiritual guidance and to open their awareness on the next level. The symbol would indicate someone who had made a major shift in thier life and thinking. I would expect the reading to unfold with ideas and suggestions for future learning, meeting new people, and making progress in all areas of life.

This symbol can also indicate a need for protection. This person may be in an abusive relationship, and perhaps I am being shown this by the appearance of the Sei He Ki—the universal symbol for protection.

How do we know the difference? We need to go with the feelings we are getting from the person and the pictures we are being shown. Does the person feel comfortable—or scared and apprehensive? People come to me up to sixteen months before they move from an abusive relationship. This is their choice, and I can only provide good advice and phone numbers for support. People in trouble have low self-esteem, and we may be able to help out by boosting their confidence.

If I am given a symbol for "clearing," I know that a person has an issue that needs to be addressed, and I may be able to help them do so. Sometimes this involves letting go or forgiving. Sometimes it means it is time for the person to move on from a relationship, a job, an area, the domination of older children, and so forth.

Space will give people time to sort themselves out, to build their confidence, and to work out the words they need to build their self-respect and improve their communication skills. Sometimes it is just an old issue that needs to be finalized and dropped. As time goes by, we sometimes make old issues into something really big, constantly holding ourselves back by thinking about them. When we take the time to deal with old issues, we can feel free and light, moving onward to the next steps on our pathways.

If your client has no interest in letting go of blockages from their chakras, this is not your business. Just continue with the reading.

If I was given a symbol for moving forward, it would be time to create a new and different reality by offering a lot of choices and challenges for the future. There are times when people will become stuck in their lives; the growth stops or slows, and they waste years living with doubt or the fear of making changes or tackling life on their own. We always have more than one path ahead of us, and we will choose the one that has the next lesson we need. Kindness and encouragement are important during readings. While you may not agree with your clients' choices, the choices are theirs to make.

If I was shown a picture of a sad child, I would know that there was a lot of inner-child work to do, addressing loneliness and a lack of confidence. Children from abusive relationships carry a lot of burdens, as do abandoned children. They often feel completely unloved and unable to give love. It is a sad and lonely journey for them. You will have the opportunity to help, support, make suggestions, listen to their fears and anger, and suggest a good counsellor for them. By talking through this troubled time, adults can move forward into happiness, new friends, and new relationships with themselves and others. This may also involve some forgiveness exercises, so make sure that you have some at hand.

The Isis Seichim symbols of the harth or a set of scales in a reading would indicate balance, harmony, and better times to come. Maybe it would be showing peace after trouble and strife, better health after illness, or a need to bring oneself back into balance and to look at a situation in a different light. It may indicate an artist with a love of beauty and harmony, who will bring gifts to many people.

These symbols could also show that a person needs some time off to bring themselves back into balance. You may need to recommend a holiday, massages, reiki treatments, spas, or special time with a loved one.

If I was continually shown Cho Ku Reis in the reading, I would know that the person was extremely fatigued. I would suggest that they go to a practitioner for some energy work to lift energy levels and vibrations. Tiredness would be paramount, and I would know to slow the reading down, as the possibility of their taking everything on-board would be slight. Tired people cannot retain everything we are saying to them. Make sure you have a note pad or tape recording for them to take with them. This symbol may also indicate that a person is a workaholic, someone who spends too many hours at work and not enough time relaxing.

If I was shown a peach-coloured rosebud, it would indicate that a pregnancy was very near. A peach-coloured rose, open and beautiful, means that a pregnancy is already happening and that the mother is blooming with good health. Remember that the pregnancy may not apply to the client; it may apply to a daughter or close friend.

It can also indicate a brilliant new idea or an idea that is already being put into practice—one that will be very successful, like an open rose.

This symbol can show a need for more sensuality in people's lives, a need to take time out to make lovemaking special. We can suggest burning essential oils in their homes, using rose or ylang-ylang or aromatherapy massage, burning scented candles, buying some sensual clothes, and so on. We can encourage these people to take time to spoil their partner—and themselves.

As you work with symbols, you will come to put your own thoughts to them. There is no right or wrong. Just go with your intuition.

Many people see golden chalices, rainbows, trees, and so on. I have given an explanation of these later in this book. However, remember that we all have our own answers and ways of working with symbols. I am only trying to give you some ideas that may prove useful in the future. Set up your own picture dictionary, and add to it regularly as you work with spirit.

CHAPTER 16

Past Lives

I find that past lives will sometimes come up in a reading. I also work with past lives as a separate therapy, but sometimes we need to release something from a past life to move forward in this life. Past lives are locked into our cells and into our psyche; they determine how we act and how we treat others at times.

We often meet people that we feel attracted to or very comfortable with—or maybe it's the opposite, and we are scared of them or uncomfortable with them. Such a feeling is often based on past life experiences with that particular person. As the reader, you may experience this with some of your clients.

Ask permission to look at a past life. The person may not be interested, or scared by the idea. Also, some people still do not believe in more than one life, so respect their wishes.

If I was shown a *past life symbol*, I would know that I needed to clear a troublesome past life—if the person was open to this.

Case Study #1

Many years ago, I worked with a lady who ran in her sleep, and this was causing problems in her relationship. Her running had been instrumental in ending her first marriage, and it was creating havoc in her second marriage. Her relationship was on the verge of collapsing.

We started working through to a relevant past life. I took her deep into a past life and asked her questions.

"Where are you?" I asked.

"In a little cottage on a hill overlooking the sea," she replied.

"Whose cottage is it?" I queried.

"It is my parents' cottage. They died, and now I am here all alone. I am only seventeen, and I am scared here by myself." She continued, "He is coming to get me. He will be here soon." Her voice shook.

"Who is coming? Who are you so scared of?"

"My neighbour. He has had three wives already, and they all died during childbirth, and he belted them when they didn't do what he told them to do. He has eleven children, and he wants me and the farm."

There was a short silence.

"Where shall I hide?" she mumbled. "Where shall I hide? He will find me, and I don't want to marry him. He is ugly, and all of his wives die. Help me. He is coming. I can hear him coming up the hill. I am going to hide now." Her voice dropped to a whisper. "He is at the door. I won't let him in."

"Help me, help me," she pleaded. "I can hear him banging and yelling. He is going to break in, and I don't know what to do. He will find me! Oh, no! Here he comes! I have to run." Suddenly she began to cry.

"What are you doing now?" I asked quietly. "Are you safe?"

"No, I am running out the door, and he is following me, yelling at me. I have to run faster." She sounded breathless. "I have to keep going. He is gaining on me. He is horrible. Oh no!" She screamed.

She was tossing in her chair. It was nearly time to bring her back. She was holding her throat and gasping for air.

"What happened?" I asked. "Did he catch you?"

"Yes," she said. "He is grabbing me around the neck and squeezing. I can't breathe. I think he is going to kill me. I am floating above my body, watching him. He is so big. He has such big hands and red hair, and his face is red from running."

"What happened next? Do you remember?" I asked.

"He kept on yelling at me, 'Don't be dead, you stupid girl!' He was shouting at me and shaking me. I was floating above my body, and I heard my mother's voice. She had come for me, and I was happy to go with her."

At this stage, I returned her to the room.

We did some clearing exercises, and she became calmer and had a greater understanding of what was happening to her.

In her current lifetime, this lady had come across this man again—and hence the need to run to keep safe from him. Even though he had a different appearance and was very civil to her in this present lifetime, her cells responded with panic, running in her sleep state.

By clearing this past life, the lady no longer ran in her sleep state. Her health picked up and the fatigue went away. Her relationship improved, and she stayed with her husband.

Case Study #2

The next case study involves a young woman who was afraid to commit in a relationship. When her relationship with a young man deepened and marriage was mentioned, she broke it off.

We went into a past life relevant to the current problem—one in which she was getting married and was very happy and very much in love.

"What can you see?" I asked her.

"It is my wedding day," she said, smiling. "I am so happy. I am going to marry and stay in this village. I will have my own home, and we will have lots of children. I love him so much."

"What does your husband look like?"

"He is very handsome. He has thick brown hair and brown eyes. He laughs a lot and plays jokes on me to make me laugh. I am so much in love with him. I am the luckiest woman in the world."

"And does he love you?"

"Oh, yes, he does. He says I bring the sunshine into his life."

"What does your future husband do?" I asked.

"He builds houses. He is a builder, and he is very good. I am so lucky to have him. We are so much in love. I have a new dress my mother helped me to sew. I look so pretty. It is nearly time for me to leave for the church," she added with a big grin. "I am at the church now, and all of my friends are here. I can't stop smiling."

"Let's move onward to a year after the wedding," I suggested.

"No, I don't want to," she said adamantly.

"Let's just have a look at what is happening in your life one year after the wedding."

"I am unhappy. I am angry, and I don't want to go anywhere."

"Where is your husband?" I asked.

"He is dead. He isn't old enough to be dead, but he is. It is all over. He left me."

"Are you alone in your house?" I inquired.

"Yes, and I don't want to talk to anyone," she replied tersely.

"Was your husband sick before he died?" I asked patiently.

"No. He fell from the church spire. He was repairing it, and he slipped. How could he do that to me? I loved him so much. Why did he want to go away from me?"

"I am sorry to hear that," I replied. "Let's look ahead to see if you find happiness again with someone else."

"No way. I will never love anyone like that again," she said definitely. "You just get hurt."

We moved ahead five years, and the lady was remarried to her husband's friend.

"Are you happy with your new husband?" I asked her.

"Maybe a little," she said sulkily. "He is all right, but I won't ever love him or he will die. At least he has a safe job on a farm."

We went ahead another five years, and then ten years. A bitterness came across her face, a look of divine discontent with her life.

"Are you still married?" I asked.

"Of course not. He left and found someone else. No one wants to say with me."

"Why do you think that is?"

"I won't love again. It hurts too much. He just moved on to someone else. Good riddance to him."

We looked at the rest of her life and found that she stayed on her own, lonely and bitter, wasting her life. She didn't have any children, and she rarely left the house except to shop.

We cleared this past life and worked with a second one in which she chose not to marry but had a lot of affairs, not committing to anyone.

"Where are you now?" I asked her.

"About to go onto the stage."

"Wonderful! What do you do on the stage?" I was interested to know.

"I sing and dance. I am really very good, you know!"

"Are you married?"

"No, and I never will be. Men just love you and leave you, so I don't want love—just company from time to time. I get lots of presents. I am lucky."

"Are your boyfriends single?"

"No, and they aren't boys. I have men for lovers and most of them are married. It is easier that way, and no one gets any silly ideas about tying me down."

We continued to clear the past lives and any lingering thought patterns that would prevent her from finding stability and happiness in her present lifetime.

I looked forward in time and saw this young lady dating a man who had brown hair and brown eyes. Going further ahead, I saw a garden wedding; and still further ahead, I saw two little girls playing on the lawn while their parents watched. I felt that her future was going to be really special, with much love and affection. Clearing away the old energy allowed her to move forward in a very positive way.

Case Study #3

Joining some family and friends for drinks and laughs while we were on holiday, I accepted a drink from a young man. Looking into his eyes, I felt enormous fear and apprehension. I felt my mind slip into another time and place where I had looked into those eyes—although a different colour—as he had me walled into the surroundings of a castle. I felt terror—and the determination not to scream or to beg. I also felt the certainty that I would die. I felt his hatred then—and his distain now, as I am slightly too 'alternative' for him to cope with. I was so shaken by this that I made an excuse to leave early to clear this past life. This person has moved on now to other people and other families, so I feel that I was given a window of opportunity to release this stale and fearful energy. It explained why I didn't like to be in an enclosed area, and I was able to clear this problem.

Case Study #4

Jill came into my healing room with a heavy dose of scepticism. She was interested in clearing some past lives but really wasn't sure if they were fact or fiction. We chatted for a little while, and when she was comfortable, we started to work.

We worked our way into the energies, and Jill found herself heading north, riding on a coach through lonely, wet, and boggy roads on her way to meet her future husband. She was twenty-three, with long brown hair and a sunny smile. She sat there, reflectively thinking about the events that had led her to being on this coach, heading into a new way of life. Her father was a heavy gambler and drinker, and she had been the wager in one of his games. She was to marry a man old enough to be her grandfather

I could feel her fear and trepidation as she obeyed her father and made her way north. All of her begging and tears had not stopped her father from sending her away.

On arriving, she was shown into a large and very cold bedroom. The housekeeper was thin and dour and was not willing to talk to the new bride. She was then taken to a large greeting hall, where she stood with tears running down her face as she married the elderly man beside her. He looked cruel and hard. He didn't greet her or make her feel in any way welcome at his house. She didn't hear him speak until he said his marriage vows and promptly told the priest to go. His voice was thin and strained, and his hands showed papery skin with huge age spots. They looked like claws to her.

The priest left, and she was on her own to cope with the night ahead. Her new husband was a brutal man who beat her, yelled at her, and finally raped her.

The beatings were to become a regular occurrence, as it appeared he couldn't have sex without the violence first.

Her life was very solitary, as the staff rarely spoke to her. The man's son came home after nearly two years and brought some friends to stay with him. They gave her only fleeting company, as she wasn't allowed to have meals with them or socialize. Some of them found her in the garden and attempted to speak to her and cheer her up. There were occasions when she was allowed to ride out, and there she met up with a particular young a man and fell in love.

Together they planned the husband's death by poisoning. As he wasn't a well man, he spent days in his bed with the doctor and retainers looking after him. The wife slipped a white powder into his goblet and fed it to him. He died, leaving her free to marry the young lover. However, fate stepped in, and the old man's son arrived to take over the establishment. He sent the woman to a nunnery for the rest of her life. The young man moved on to a new conquest when he realized there wouldn't be any money or future with his lover.

The young woman spent many unhappy years, thinking about the three men who had controlled her life: her father, her husband, and her lover, all of whom had let her down.

In this present lifetime, she had a fear of men and a great need to be independent and make her own choices. She could not tolerate touch and abhorred violence. She needed to release this past life in order to move forward.

We released her fear of betrayal and gave her the opportunity to move forward with grace.

CHAPTER 17

Preparing to Work

I like to prepare the room I will be working in, filling it with lovely, bright, white light and reiki and Seichim symbols. I like to have the oil burner going to create ambience in the room and to have a few minutes to quiet my mind and call in my spirit helpers. I ask for help during the reading, for my thoughts to be clear and accurate, and for anyone from spirit who wishes to give a message to come through clearly to me so I can make the connection.

I add the following colours to the room: pink for unconditional love, blue to enhance my communication skills and to make my clients feel comfortable with me, green for balance, and a little violet to help me to transmute any negativity that may come up during the reading. The room looks to me as if it filled with soft, gentle colours—like the ones reflected from stained glass with the sunlight behind them.

I have crystals in my reading room at home, and I enjoy the energy from them. Flowers also add to the room and give everyone much pleasure. Scented candles also add ambience.

While none of these things are must-haves, I enjoy preparing to work and taking my thoughts away from my everyday matters. Meditation leads me into a place of quiet contemplation. Your own preparation is entirely up to you, as we all create our own ways to work in service for spirit.

I am at all times conscious of the karmic debt created by reading for others, so I try to be positive, helpful, and accurate with the messages I pass on. I prefer not to start bringing in the information until my client has arrived. This is my personal choice. You need to work the way that suits you best. Be aware that not everyone has had a reading or a good experience in a reading, so let kindness light your day.

If you are doing mediumship, you will need to know if you are speaking to the spirit of a man or a woman. Then try to give several pieces of evidence to your client, as well as personal messages. Spirit guides often touch your shoulder or your hair, and they may touch your clients so they can feel them.

Sometimes they create a feeling of pins and needles, and more often than not, they make the hairs on your arms stand up. This also happens to me when I strike a home run in my readings; it validates what I am saying. Sometimes you just get a feeling that the spirit person is older, like a grandparent or parent, or is a similar age, like a sibling, cousin, or friend. Children hold different energy—often light and bubbly—and they are lovely to chat to.

Some spirit guides bring the aroma of flowers or cigars. Sometimes you will smell their favourite perfume or aftershave. Good cooks will give you a whiff of hot apple pie, hot bread, or your favourite food. Some will give you a number, which may represent the date they passed—called their "anniversary" in spirit—or a significant birthday for themselves or for someone in their family. You may be shown new babies, a completed novel, or a new residence. Be aware that at all times you will be given signals and symbols from spirit.

You may experience pain in some part of your body as spirit people convey to you what they had wrong with them when they passed over. At times I have experienced difficulty in breathing, chest pain, head pain, and difficulty swallowing—among other symptoms.

These people from spirit will come with love. If you work with wonderful, positive energy, it is easier for them to pass messages through you to their loved ones.

Many are very witty, and you may hesitate at times to pass on their mischievous messages. However, these messages are very important to the recipient. It validates who the message came from, as no other words could.

I have a brother and father in spirit, as well as my grandparents and a very special aunt, and I do receive messages from them. They are present at family Christmases, birthdays, and all special occasions. They are still very interested in our earthly lives.

I would like to give you some case studies so that you will know what to expect—although you should always expect the unexpected.

Case Study #1

I was busy ironing one day, when I had a visitor who was thinking about learning Isis Seichim with me, so I had the opportunity to explain the lovely, gentle, healing modality to her.

While we were talking, a young man approached me from spirit, saying, "Tell mum I am sorry I was such a shit."

"No way," was my answer. He persisted with just that comment.

"I will tell her that you love her," I said to him.

"She knows that," he said. "Just give her the message.

I said no several times over the next twenty minutes, but he persisted and nearly drove me mad. I really didn't know his mum well enough to know how she would cope with this message.

He showed me his death, which really upset me, and I decided to just pass on the message. I am so glad that I did—exactly as he said it—as it was significant to both of them.

This lady is now a special friend, and I have passed on many messages over the years to her from her cheeky son.

Over the years, I had to drive many hours to reach my new friend's house, where I would visit and do readings. On the cupboard, "our lad" had a photo of himself with a white background. As I got closer to my friend's house, the background in the photo would turn pink. By the time I arrived, it was quite a dark pink, so I could never sneak up to surprise that family. Many visitors to the house saw this happen over the years.

This lady's son brought to me the important lesson of repeating a message exactly as it is given to me—not to make changes, soften it, or alter it in any way.

Case Study #2

I have a friend who has a son in spirit. One night when we were sitting and chatting after a long and tiring day, he popped in to say hello to his mum.

"Hi, sweetheart," I said in my head. "Could you possibly come back in the morning? I am really tired now."

"Can't I just say hello?" he asked.

"Not really," I told him, "as you always want to say more, and I really am past it for tonight."

"Okay," he answered.

The next thing I knew, I was seeing lots of mangoes: sliced, diced, on salad platters, hanging in the trees—over and over, mangoes everywhere. It was very distracting, and I missed some of what my friend was saying.

After a while, my friend asked what I was seeing, because I really wasn't paying attention to her.

"Mangoes," I replied. "Lots and lots of mangoes."

She started to laugh, saying, "My son has been here, hasn't he?"

I said, "Yes, he did pop in."

"And you sent him away until later?" She laughed.

"Yes, I did."

"Well, you wouldn't know this, as he died before you and I met, but his nickname was Mango. So he has my attention anyway."

Cheeky, these young men in spirit!

Case Study #3

Many years ago, I had the opportunity to read for a friend who had no real belief or disbelief in spirit. I read his watch for a couple of hours and found out a lot of personal information for him concerning his father and the family Bible. Much of the information was verified over the next few weeks, giving this gentleman an insight into his family. He had messages from departed friends, but mainly it was family information. Spirit also mentioned a speeding ticket on the way home from my place, which was avoided due to spirit's timely intervention. I later heard that many of the things mentioned in the reading had been validated.

Case Study #4

I recently had a message from my father, who told me that I was working too hard, trying too hard to please everyone. He also pointed out that I had lost my sense of humour and that he wanted me to get it back and laugh a lot more like I used to. So you see, even from spirit, parents are watching, encouraging, and keeping us on track.

Case Study #5

One night I was cooking a roast dinner for my friend, and in came his mother from spirit to tell me just how he liked his vegetables done. "He likes his roast potatoes crunchy," she told me, "and with gravy. I will show you how to arrange it on the plate."

I was thinking that I had made many roasts in my time—especially when I was a cook in the outback for several years, cooking for station hands and shearers—but I did as she asked, and we chatted away while I worked. I found her to be delightful, and when I put the meal on the table, she was happy with it.

My friend took one look and said, "This looks just like my mother cooked dinner. She knew just how I liked it."

Well, he was right. She sure did. I now see his mother on a regular basis and enjoy her helpful kitchen hints—especially the ones that say "Quick, Trish, something is burning!"

Case Study #6

My mother recently moved to Queensland from South Australia. We searched for suitable units for her and found one we liked in a retirement village. The real estate agent offered us a thick book of rules for the establishment, but he said he didn't think there would be anything interesting in it. By this time, I was feeling sick, my spiritual barometer indicating that something was very wrong here.

Returning home, I read the book and found that if mum went into that particular village and then died, a big percentage of the price of the unit would go to the establishment. As her will would leave the unit to me and my brother, we would also have to pay the same amount again to sell it. The family would receive just over half the value of the unit. This was not what my mother wanted, as my parents had worked hard for their money and wanted to keep their nest egg in the family.

So, do not ignore this type of feeling. If you feel sick, uncomfortable, or restless, look deeper into the situation. All may not be as it appears. Mum went on to find a lovely unit with large rooms and a lovely little garden.

Case Study #7

Sometimes when you read, the reading is just to validate the love coming from spirit. I am given fairly ordinary information, from and about the person who has passed over. When reading for an elderly and charming gentleman, I was given a picture of his wife's favourite chair, a place where he now sits to be close to her. His wife wanted him to move closer to family so he wasn't so lonely.

Material Values

Some messages are from children who are just sending their love and letting their parents know that they are okay in their new lives. Eager, bright voices in my ear, they reassure us all that they have another life in a different dimension.

Children who come in and go out quickly often do so to teach their parents that money and prestige are not everything. Love is what our existence is all about: compassion, understanding, warmth, caring, and grace. If you do not have the joy of your child's arms around your neck, it doesn't matter how expensive your house and car are.

The values people place on the material world are illusion. It is the heart energies that unite us with our totality and with our soul groups. We are simply asked to be the best people we can be, to offer kindness and compassion to everyone who crosses our path. Spirit world really isn't interested in how much our jeans cost or who has the biggest house, and we certainly won't be taking any of these things with us when we go home to another dimension. Our homes in the next dimension are built according to how we live our lives here on earth, and there isn't a monetary system there.

We are experiencing a time when the energies are changing rapidly. People who did not have any awareness of energy and spirit ten years ago are asking many questions.

Here are some of the questions I am asked.

Is this all there is?

No, it certainly isn't. This is just one level of learning. The earth journey is important, but certainly it is not the only level of existence.

Why do I need to learn these things?

We are here to enhance our personal growth, the growth of our soul group, and ultimately the growth of our monad. Through adversity we strengthen ourselves and become at peace with ourselves. Much growth also comes from healing ourselves and others as we learn to work with the energy coming to this planet. We are here to learn empathy and compassion and to connect to the animal kingdom, nature, and the nature spirits. There are so many lessons for us to work our way through to help us reconnect to our true selves. We need to live this life with genuine intention to better ourselves and to be proud of the progress we are making. All life is sacred, and we each have a sacred contract we made in spirit to fulfil. Our life is an incredible gift; we need to live it with appreciation and with a positive attitude.

When do I get to use the things I learn?

Every day, in every way, show kindness and love to yourself and others. Be proud of who you are, be helpful toward others, and work with positive energy. Practice forgiveness; this heart energy is really important. Accept challenge as an opportunity for making new decisions with perceptiveness.

Is there some value in meditating?

There is a lot of value in meditating. You can learn how to still your mind, speak to your spirit guides, go to other dimensions, and learn to be part of the bigger picture. Meditation relieves stress and helps your physical body to heal.

Are the messages from spirit real?

Yes, they are. Your spirit guides—when you have correctly connected to them—will only give you the truth. Errors come in when you are not making a sound connection and begin using your imagination. Guesses are not from spirit.

Is there life after death?

There is no death. We are energy, and therefore we cannot die. We can only transmute into a different form. Think of water turning into steam. Our soul is eternal, so the journey continues in a different place.

Where do we go to when we leave this planet?

We go to the fourth dimension, to the plane where our family—or people at a similar level of advancement—go. There are many different levels, some with great beauty and huge schools of music, healing, and learning.

How do you know who is talking to you?

It takes practice and dedication to work the energies until you have a good connection. When you connect to your guide, your feelings are wonderful. You feel the love.

Why do I get on well with some people and not others?

This is often karmic. You may have had problems with people in other lifetimes, and your energy body remembers this. You may have been married to the person or loved them as your child, which will bring back the love this time around.

Do people view their own funerals?

Yes, we are given the opportunity to view our funerals. We can see who genuinely cared for us in this lifetime, and know who we have hurt or upset. It is a great opportunity to learn and to correct any errors we may have made. The funeral may be viewed at the time it occurs—or later when we are ready to reconnect with our earth family and friends.

How long are we in spirit before we return to earth?

This varies greatly. Sometimes it is not long at all, and other times many years pass before you are ready to come back—usually with your soul group for your next lot of lessons.

Do we go to other planets to learn?

I have been told by my spiritual teachers that it is possible for us to go to other planets to learn. It depends on our own spiritual development.

When you refer to "spirit," what do you mean?

When I refer to spirit, I am talking about anyone who has passed from this planet. I can be referring to a single entity or a group of teachers.

When you refer to the "soul," what do you mean?

We all have a soul: the inner expression of everything we are, have been, and will be. This is your essence. You will have heard the expression that you are a beautiful soul, meaning that you shine on the inside and are kind and caring toward everyone. Your soul is eternal. It is the flame in your heart that is with you always, through all of your incarnations and in every dimension you go to. You cannot die, because your soul is eternal.

CHAPTER 18

Aspects of Your Client's Personality

It is a help if you have done some archetypal work or read some books on the archetypes. It will give you insight into the person who is sitting opposite you. You can discuss archetypal work with your guides during meditation. It is also advantageous to take some counselling courses, as your advice should be sound and based on facts as well as your intuition. If you are a responsible reader, you will want to do the best job you can to help your client.

It is handy to have a list of people your clients can go to for help, including doctors with an understanding of energy, welfare people, counsellors, accountants, financial investors, meditation classes, reiki teachers, massage therapists, aroma therapists, naturopaths, astrologers, homeopaths, reflexologists, and so on.

Let's have a look at some of the aspects you will see in a reading. People may change, depending on various factors—whether they like what you are saying, are offended by your honesty, are ready for your information, or suddenly feel accountable if you mention their spirit guides. I make it a practice not to read for young people under eighteen years of age, unless they have a parent with them and the reading is based on healing. This is a personal choice, and I am rarely asked to read for young people.

The Child Persona

How do you recognize the child persona during readings?

On the negative side, the child persona chats a lot to distract you when you get into the serious stuff. People with this persona pull a lot of faces, look for attention, and talk more than you do. They look for approval. They want you to tell them exactly what it is they want to resolve.

These people don't care if you tell the truth; they just want you to say what they want to hear. They tell you that others don't listen to them or treat them with respect. They tell you things a half dozen times and have questions long after you have finished, even though you have probably addressed them earlier in the reading. They get cross with you for not telling them they are victims, and they do not take responsibility for their lives. They do not listen to most of what you say.

On the positive side, people with the child persona are fun and very likable. They show lots of potential when they are ready to make life-changing shifts. They are usually kind and considerate toward others. Often they are wide-eyed and have good skin and a youthful appearance. They appreciate their spirit guides coming through with encouragement and messages, and they are very excited to hear from loved ones.

Keep in mind that people are sometimes unaware of their childlike behaviour, and when you politely point it out, they simply stop. Others are annoyed and belligerent, as their actions usually work with everyone else. We all do what works for us, so if their childlike behaviour is considered cute and funny by their friends and family, they will continue to do it. It often helps them to get their own way, acting like they don't understand when they really do. They can use this behaviour to get sympathy or to have someone answer all of their questions so they do not have to front up and act responsibly. This can be very amusing in a reading, but it is not very productive.

You can encourage such people to take responsibility and to see life through more mature eyes, but the choice is up to them. A sulky child is much more of a problem, and the sulkiness often starts when you start to tell truths that they don't want to face at that time in their lives. They are too immature to accept your comments in the spirit in which they are given, and they decide that resentment and not communicating with you is the way to go.

On the other hand, have fun with the positive child persona. The delightful, happy child persona is a joy to work with. You can share their enthusiasm for life, and they are open to every bit of information. They laugh and smile and are genuinely happy people.

The Saboteur Persona

How do you recognize the saboteur persona during a reading? These people have had a multitude of opportunities but continually shoot themselves in the foot. They are afraid to go ahead with a good idea, usually giving it to someone else and then complaining that the idea was stolen. When doors open for them, they refuse to see the opportunity, or they think someone else could do the job better. They often think they are not good enough for good things to happen to them, and they choose not to believe the good things you tell them. They continually feed you negativity, as they are lacking confidence and self-esteem. They cannot accept compliments, because they have not been brought up with praise and they don't know their worth. They tell you they are not ready to make change because change wouldn't work for them. They suffer with stress and maybe stomach ulcers. They are restless in your company. They apologize for taking up your time and then start their story again.

When the saboteur appears, you have the opportunity to build their confidence, mention their wonderful, positive attributes, and encourage them toward success. Sometimes a kind word does wonders in helping this person to find their true value. You can dissuade this person from giving away good ideas and can refer them to appropriate help or professional advice. Everyone needs someone to believe in them and to give them encouragement.

The Victim Persona

How do you recognize the victim persona during a reading?
These people blame everyone else for their misfortunes. They believe that someone has stolen their man/woman or cheated

to get the new job. Their parents are at fault for their personal problems. Their siblings are the reason they are unhealthy, unlucky, or missing out on golden opportunities. It's their partner's fault that the marriage didn't work. It's their business partner's fault that the business is not doing well. They cannot see that they are drowning in negativity, and they do not want to see and take responsibility for their own lives. They often have big health issues.

Deal with the victim mentality by gently leading such people into seeing that many of their own decisions led them to you. They had free will. They had the choice to do things differently. When they were in spirit, they set up the families they would learn from and the people who would be main players in their lives. Explain to them that some lessons are easy and others are hard, but they are all sent to make us develop—and most importantly, they are the lessons we chose for ourselves.

Ask these "victims" to turn their comments around and look at them from a different perspective. Help them to take responsibility for their lives and the choices they have made and will be making. Teach them how to make good decisions and to look at life as a wonderful experience filled with learning lessons that they can cope with.

The Lover/Player Persona

How do you recognize the lover persona during a reading?

On the positive side, these people see a world filled with beauty that is not dependent on good looks but on good energy. They see the best in everyone around them and are kind and affectionate to those in their lives. They are not afraid of commitment; they see it as an opportunity for growth with a partner. Sending out love from warm and caring hearts, they understand that unconditional love is there for all of us, and they back this with kindness and compassion. The positive lover can see within to the beauty that resides in another person's heart.

On the negative side, these people are on a continual quest to find perfect love, and they do not see any fault in themselves. They boast that the opposite sex hits on them all the time. They think they can have anyone they want, without looking at the consequences, and they are open to affairs with married people. Although they have many lovers, they are never content, and each relationship is only good at the beginning. When the flame dies, they move on—often before ending the previous relationship. They insist on good looks and good performance in bed, and they are shallow in their affections. These people may fall in and out of love easily, as they are always looking for something that is just out of their reach. They may require a young partner, so they can be the mentor in the relationship. These lovers may have had lots of relationships—or they may not have had any relationships, because they are too fussy, always looking for perfection in their partners.

I think this is the most difficult persona in a reading, as it is very difficult to help the negative lover want to make different choices. You can never change anything for another person; you can only offer suggestions giving them different points of view.

You will realize by now that all of these personas can come with one person to a reading, and possibly many more. Be aware of which one you are talking to at any time. You can deflect negativity and turn it into a positive outcome with some hard work and caring.

CHAPTER 19

Training Exercises for the Reader

P sychic and intuitive training is enhanced by regular mental exercises that lift your energies and give you confidence and accuracy.

Before you start working, remember to call in your guide to assist you. Some of these exercises are more beneficial if you work with a friend.

Yes/No Cards

Cut white poster cardboard into eight-centimetre squares. Write *yes* on half of your cards and *no* on the other half. You will only be working with one set of cards, so you have a fifty percent chance of getting it right. Place two cards—one yes and one no—face down on the table. Mix them around several times with your eyes closed. Keep changing hands and directions with the cards, and then try to find the yes card. Continue to do this exercise until you are very proficient at finding the card you are seeking. Alternatively, close your eyes and move the cards around the table, and then ask a question. Concentrate on the question, and then select a card for your answer. Record your progress, as you will work on easy questions to begin with.

Coloured Cards

You will need a sheet of white poster cardboard, six sheets of different-coloured, plain wrapping paper, glue, a pencil, and a glass.

Using the glass and pencil, draw six circles about six centimetres in diameter on each colour of the wrapping paper. Cut them out and put them to one side. Now, rule the white poster cardboard into eight-centimetre squares and cut them out—one for each coloured circle. Glue one coloured disc onto each square of white cardboard, and leave them all to dry. When they are dry, they are ready to use. You will use this set of six cards, each displaying one of the six colours represented, for the four exercises below.

Exercise #1

Shuffle the cards with the colour facing away from you. Choose one card and place it upside down on the table in front of yourself. Ask spirit to help you to identify the colour. Turn the card over and see if you were correct. Do this exercise ten times, recording your accuracy. You will improve with practice.

Exercise #2

Place your six cards on the table with the colours concealed. Choose a colour, concentrate, and find it. After each choice, shuffle the cards or move them around. Do this exercise ten to twenty times and record your accuracy.

Exercise #3

Make a list of your colours. Shuffle your cards with the colours concealed. Lay them out in their shuffled order, and then turn them over to see if you have laid them out in the order you wrote on your list. Work until you have ten correct matches.

Exercise #4

Work with a friend. Ask your friend to choose a coloured card and hold it against his or her heart or third eye and project the colour to you. Make two guesses, and if you aren't correct, ask your friend to change the card to a different colour. Do this exercise ten times. Record your progress.

Symbols Cards (based on the Zenner cards)

With this exercise, you can use four or six different symbols to work the exercises above to get clarity and accuracy. You will need a sheet of white poster cardboard and a marking pen. Rule up the cardboard into squares of eight or ten centimetres, and then draw one symbol on each card, such as: waves, circle, square, triangle, diamond, rectangle, star, pentagon, octagon, etc. Use these cards to repeat the exercises listed under coloured cards.

Cards with Positive Words

Make more white cardboard cards and write a positive word on each one. Chose from the following: peace, love, harmony, balance, faith, hope, courage, grace, integrity, wisdom, forgiveness, and kindness. You can also choose your own words. Working with four cards, find the word you are searching for. As you get better at this exercise, write down the words you use, so you use different words at different times.

Cards with Numbers

Using the white poster cardboard again, place a number on each of your cards. Work with numbers one to four until you are confident, and then add two numbers at a time until you have ten numbers. Work with these ten cards until you are scoring at least seven out of a possible ten.

The exercises below are simple, but you will need to put time in to gain accuracy.

Seek and Find: House

In this exercise you will be working with a friend. Ask your friend to go to a room in your house and stay there for five minutes. You are to go outside, sit quietly, and ask spirit which room your friend is in. After five minutes, your friend will come and find you, and you can tell your friend where they were hiding in the house. Do this exercise several times.

Seek and Find: Garden

It is now your turn to sit in the house while your friend finds a place to stand in the garden or shed. After five minutes, they will return, and you can tell where they were standing in the garden.

Phone Exercises

1. Try remote viewing. Phone a friend and ask him or her to go to a room in their house. Do you know which room they are in?
2. Ask your friend to phone you when they are out and about, and try to work out where your friend is by asking your guides for the information.
3. Phone a friend and ask them to place an item on their dining room table. Phone back within five minutes, when you have worked out what the item is.
4. Phone a friend and instruct them to write someone's name on a piece of paper and place it on the dining room table. Take five minutes, and then phone back with your choice of name.
5. Phone a friend and tell them what they are wearing or what they were doing when you phoned.

Try all of these versions many times until you become very accurate. You can create many different exercises from these basic ones.

Sensing Energy

Exercise #1

Go to a friend's house, where you have some of your friends plus some strangers waiting in a room where you cannot see them. Stand in a room by yourself and place a dark blindfold over your eyes.

One by one, these people will quietly come into the room and stand in front of you. Tell them if they are male or female, and if you know who it is, name the person. If you are a medium, you may have some words for them from spirit or messages from those who have passed over. Ask your friend to record your answers, as you will not take off the blindfold until you have finished. Check your accuracy.

Exercise #2

For this exercise, you will be working with two groups of people. Line up some chairs and have half the people leave the room. Have the others sit on the chairs, wearing blindfolds and facing a wall.

The first group of people will come into the room and place their hands on the shoulders of those sitting. The people on the chairs will be doing the readings, so give them time to amass some information. Then, one by one, ask a blindfolded person to read aloud to the person standing behind. Do not take off any blindfolds or give any information to the readers until everyone has read.

When everyone has read, the blindfolds can come off, and they can discuss their findings. Keep things light, as they have all done their best.

Exercise #3

Stand in the middle of a circle of people with a blindfold on. One by one, these people will quietly leave the room until only one person is left. Work out who is still in the room with you, tell the person who you think they are, and then take off your blindfold.

Exercise #4

You will work with spirit people for this exercise. Ask spirit if you could please feel the energy of females on your right side and males on your left side. Take some time for them to work with you with this exercise. Practice every day until you are confident.

Exercise #5

You will need sheets of paper, envelopes, and a pen. Write a number onto each piece of paper, fold them all well, and place each one in a separate envelope. Work with the numbers one through twenty. (You can use the numbers more than once, as you will need enough envelopes for one month of training.) Each day, choose an envelope and write down the number you think is within. Open and check the number, and then record your accuracy rate.

You can repeat the above exercise with colours, photos, or pictures cut out of magazines.

Yes/No Answers from Spirit

Focus on the middle of your forehead. Feel your thoughts. Thoughts have energy.

Move your thoughts to the left-hand side of your forehead. Did you feel the energy move? Now move your thoughts to the right-hand side of your forehead, and you should feel the energy move across. Shift your energy several times, and then move the energy back to the centre of your forehead.

Now, ask spirit to move the energy to the left, indicating a *no* answer, and then to the right, indicating a *yes* answer.

If you put the time in to get this exercise right, this will be invaluable to you when you are doing a reading.

Working with Your Future

Make a list of ten questions that pertain to your next three months, and work out your *yes* or *no* answers. Keep an eye on this list and check your accuracy against what actually occurs.

On another list, ask questions whose answers will unfold over the next year. This is a great way to work with yes/no answers and to improve your accuracy.

Simple Daily Exercises

Always work out who is calling before you answer the *phone*, and if there is time, determine what they want to speak to you about.

Before checking your *emails* every morning, work out who your emails are from and how many there are to start your day.

When going through your *mail*, hold each letter in your hands and work out the contents. If you are holding a bill, work out the amount of the bill, and write the amount on the outside of the envelope. If it is a letter, work out who it is from and what their main news is. If it is advertising, try to feel or see what is being advertised.

Watch a *game show* every day or week, and work out who will win or who will be evicted. Record your answers and check your accuracy. Talent shows and competitive cooking shows are also excellent for this exercise.

If you have a *baby or toddler*, look at the time your child goes to sleep during the day, and write down what time you think they will awaken.

Before you go to *work*, record what colour tie your boss will be wearing for the day, or the colour of the secretary's clothes. There's a multitude of details you can record while having your breakfast, and then you can check your accuracy when you get home at night. You will improve and feel much more confident with your intuition.

You can ask your guide *basic questions* before your client arrives. These might include the person's age, job, interests, and—if you are doing mediumship—messages from loved ones.

CHAPTER 20

Reading Flowers

Flowers come in so many different varieties and colours. They can be delicate, robust, fragrant, and aromatic. They are a delight to behold—and to do readings with. Flowers make wonderful gifts and decorations in our homes and gardens.

Flowers can be read in psychic and intuitive development classes or in actual readings.

When people hand you a flower to read, they will have chosen a flower that suits them and their story at that time. They will be drawn to the correct flower for you to read, and often it is not the flower they had originally chosen to bring to you. This flower will give you their vibrations after they have held it, and the structure and colour of the flower itself will produce thoughts and feelings.

As with all of the readings discussed in this book, I am sharing with you my ideas and suggestions. If you are not comfortable with my methods, please move on to the next section. Once you start to read using the suggestions offered in this book, you will find that your intuition will take you to many different ideas and areas to help others. The most important thing is to work with a kind and open heart.

Hold the flower in your hands, close your eyes, and let the images form in your head. How do you feel about them? Are you feeling happy, sad, hopeful? Let your thoughts wander before you start work. Make notes or share your feelings with your client.

Look at the stems. Are they long or short? What does this mean to you? A long stem may indicate a laid-back person who takes time to think things over. A short stem implies a more impatient person, one who is short on time and very busy. Add your own thoughts to every list you make.

What colour is the stem? Is it vibrant green, indicating freshness, vibrancy, and lots of new ideas? Or is it dull green, which sometimes shows tiredness, a nervous disposition, or envy? Your client may have lots of ideas but not enough energy to see projects through. Grey-green would indicate someone who stays in the background and is not a good communicator. Brown denotes an earthy person who resonates with Mother Nature, the environment, and the animal kingdom. This person is grounded and reliable.

Every colour takes you into different thoughts. Each time you work, you will find your thoughts heading in different directions. If you get stuck, head into what you know about the chakras. This will open you to new thoughts and ideas.

Does the stem look strong? If the stem is straight, you may be looking at someone who has a strong and capable personality, someone who may be walking a straight path and is capable of helping others. See if you can feel anything new coming up for them. Will there be a job, a new house, or new projects? Do you feel that this person has the strength of character to overcome illness or disadvantages? Do you feel this person may be a little stubborn or controlling? Do you think this person may be a very good provider? Is he/she strait-laced? Do you need to put a lid on your own sense of humour while working with them? Would you find this person to be dependable? Would you expect them to have a responsible job? Are they suited to leadership?

Is the stem weak? Do you feel that the person has a weaker character or is ill or overpowered by someone close by? The stem may give you a flat or sinking feeling or a sense of being unappreciated. If it is very floppy, is there a confidence issue here? Has the person come out of an unhappy relationship, feeling lonely and unable to cope? Does the person have a victim mentality? Are they bereaved? Depressed? Do they have a controlling parent or partner? Are they unhappy at work? Can you suggest positive changes?

Is the stem flexible? A flexible stem indicates a flexible mind and a person who is open to changes and is willing to learn new things. Do you feel new offers coming in for this person? Do you think this person is the peacemaker in their family? Do you think the person is not easily ruffled? Do you feel a great sense of humour and/or ability to overcome life's tests? Do you feel that this person would be very popular? Do you feel they can learn through travel? Is this person happy in social situations? Is stress handled well?

Is the stem very rigid? Sometimes when a person picks a rigid stem, it shows they have been brought up with very narrow views. You need to learn if this is still the case in their adult life. Is this person unyielding? Does the person listen to other points of view? Are they open to change? Do they have a very religious background? Is this person very strict with his/her children? What are some of their big fears? Do they feel unloved? Are you making this person nervous? Can you put them at ease?

Are there any thorns or prickles? Thorns and prickles may show a prickly disposition, or someone who is easily hurt and who may speak sharply. Prickly stems can indicate times of great difficulty in people's lives. These people may have had problems with individuals in the workplace or a difficult parent. They could be in—or recently have left—an abusive or unhappy marriage. They may be prickly about starting again, not wanting to be hurt by anyone else. There may also be a prickly boss in a workplace, and if this is the case, you can try to soften the client's attitude. People with prickly stems may also be intensely private, worried about what you will read to them.

Is the stem rough? This would indicate a rough life with lots of problems that started in a person's youth. Maybe there were discipline problems with parents, lack of love, lack of food, or lack of shelter and comfort. The stem could show that this person has had a rough deal in a relationship. Use your intuition to see which way your thoughts go. Your client may be experiencing financial difficulties or undergoing serious stress. They may be rough-spoken but very kind-hearted. Are the clients mistakes repetitive? If so, you may be able to offer solutions to help make changes.

Is the stem smooth? If the stem is smooth, this person has a balanced life. They are basically happy. The immediate path ahead looks good, and they possess the skills needed at this time to have a good life. This person would be calm and relaxed, looking forward to the reading as a positive experience. They may have inner peace and be a healer, counsellor, or giver of wisdom.

How do you feel when you are holding the flower? Let some words run through your head. Get into your feelings, and use your clairsentience at this stage.

Are you feeling heavy, tired, happy, free, busy, weighed down with responsibilities, calm, anxious, or excited? Talk to your client about how you are feeling while holding their flower.

Feel and look at the flower. Write down what you can about what the *colour* means to you in this instance.

Think of some words for these colours: *yellow* (happy, optimistic, confident), *red* (energetic, motivated, ambitious), *blue* (good communicator, important news coming), *green* (calm, capable, interested in learning), *orange* (creative imagination, good sportsperson, artist), *purple* (spiritual, loyal, honest, high integrity, helpful to others).

Feel the texture. A soft but pliable flower would indicate that the person who brought the flower is kind-hearted, open to new ideas, and stronger emotionally than they look. A wilting and tired flower would indicate that the person is running on empty, and you could suggest that they take a break or do some stress management, including meditation. Stiff, waxy flowers may indicate a person who finds it difficult to communicate with others. They may have fixed ideas and find it very challenging to make changes. The person may prefer to spend a lot of time alone, or the circumstances in their life could be very trying at this time.

How much support can you see under the flower's head? The base may be strong and healthy, indicating a lot of good support in life. This person is strong and independent and would be a good friend and advisor. If the flower's support is weak and barely holding the flower together, it may indicate a person who feels alone and unsupported.

Look at the leaves. Dead leaves mean that it's time for this person to let go of something or someone who is holding him back from attaining their dreams. If the leaves are bright-green, you could predict new growth through lessons that are coming to the person; new studies, new people, and new and exciting experiences are on their way. Lots of leaves indicate busy times ahead, lots of people around, and good social times. This person is able to accomplish anything. A flower with only one leaf would tell you that the person may be stuck or lonely, unsure of the direction their life is heading. Dull-green leaves explain the person's life at this time. Prickly leaves mean that the person is definitely not happy, that they are speaking sharply to others, and may feel like a victim.

How vibrant is the flower? Does it look fresh? Do you feel vibrancy and enthusiasm? Is this person eager to start each new day? Are they open to new romance, new studies, new challenges? Do they have a positive attitude toward life? Do you feel that the person is stressed? Do you sense ill health? Is this person feeling flat and unable to cope with the current situation? How open is the recipient to what you have to say?

A Sample Flower Reading

As an exercise, let's do a sample reading of a pink pansy with a soft yellow centre.

The stem on this pansy is flexible and fragile. What would this indicate to you? We could be looking at someone who has a problem holding personal boundaries and is possibly at the beck and call of others. This person may try to please others by putting their own needs last.

The flower is delicate, fragile, and beautiful. It may feel like it is full of grace and wonderful to behold, or it may feel unsure and unsafe in the world. If the latter is so, you would look for problems like broken relationships, recovery from an illness, a need for love and affection, or a lack of confidence.

The pink colour would show a person with love and compassion in their heart, someone who may care for children or elderly parents. This person would give of their time and energy to help others. They would be warm and reliable.

The yellow centre shows vulnerability. This person may work until they drop, or be stressed or worried about others. You would encourage this person to meet some of their own needs and to make time to recharge their own batteries—with some treats or relaxation. Build this person's confidence while they are in front of you. It would be very easy to list their good qualities. Give this person encouragement and self-empowerment.

Roses *with* Thorns and Leaves

Stems with thorns would indicate that a person is strong and able to hold their boundaries. They may be sharp-spoken and rigid in their attitudes. They may show a different, more caring side of their personality to those they love. Alternatively the client may also just be intensely private.

A *white* rose indicates a very spiritual person who works and lives with integrity and honesty. A strong connection to the angelic realms and to their own spiritual guides would be evident. Possibly they work with charities or with the environment.

A *yellow* rose indicates a soft-hearted person who is gentle and loving, able to maintain cheerfulness and to respect the paths of others. They may have a great sense of humour and be very popular.

A *pink* rose indicates a caring person who may even work in the healing field. Love of family is indicated, as is consideration for others. This person makes an excellent partner and enjoys doing lovely things for others. This person's manner is graceful and nonintrusive.

A *mauve* rose would be chosen by a spiritual person with high levels of integrity. They may be multi-sensory and interested in the mysteries life has to offer. They could be resilient and very intuitive.

An *apricot* or *peach-coloured* rose shows great creativity or fertility. This shows a strong artistic streak and an open and inquiring mind. This person looks on the bright side of life and enjoys social times with friends. They are passionate and likely to experiment with all aspects of their life.

An *orange* rose would indicate an active person who may be very good at sports—and competitive in all areas of their life. This person would be sensual and sexual and great fun to be with.

A *red* rose is the vibrant colour of assertiveness. It can show strong determination and a need for attention. This person would be vigorous, grounded, and helpful, especially toward family and friends. This colour shows strong ambition and the ability to be self-motivated.

Keep in mind that rose *buds* indicate new beginnings, pregnancy, and wonderful new ideas.

Roses *without* Thorns and Leaves

Roses without thorns and leaves imply vulnerability—or maybe just a very calm person who enjoys life and lives without creating drama.

Look to see how strong the stem is. Does this person have far vision? Do they reach for the stars? Are they fulfilling their dreams? Do they have the confidence and sense of self to make their dreams come true? If the stem is short, perhaps this person is held back by another person, circumstances at work, or their own lack of initiative.

Foliage indicates protection and new growth, and lush leaves show that there is a lot of growth going on. Dead leaves need to be removed, as they indicate that a lesson has been completed and the person is ready to move on to the next set of lessons. Tiny leaves show the very beginning of an idea. Lots of leaves can indicate that the person has a lot of loving, caring people around them.

Other Common Flowers

Here are some thoughts on other common flowers that tell us a lot about the person we are reading for.

The *carnation* indicates that a person may be shy, although likes to be with friends and family. This person is often happy letting others do the talking for them. They will have a gentle inner beauty and the potential to shine in certain areas of life. This person may be refined, have good taste, and like to dress well. They may have a love of music, colour, and balanced décor. Check the colour of the flower to give yourself more hints.

Anyone presenting a *bottle brush* would have a natural self-defence and could be strongly opinionated, blunt in their speech, and at times very private. This person may be going through a difficult patch in their life at this time. There is a possibility that they may have been hurt recently and as a result protective of their own feelings now. They may have lots of responsibilities and not enough time for personal needs.

Anyone presenting a *daffodil* would have strong positive emotions and would be confident and well-balanced. They like to laugh and have good social times. The daffodil has a large listening tube in the center of the flower, so the enquirer would have the ability to listen intently to others. We could wish that people would take more notice of this person's opinions, as they would be very sound. This would be a happy-go-lucky person, a good public speaker, and an intelligent person who is looking to learn new things. Having an interest in travel and new places, this cheerful person learns a lot from foreign cultures, an explorer at heart.

A *lily* would be presented by someone who is calm and serene in times of trouble. They would have a peaceful persona, so you would feel comfortable taking your troubles to them. They would be quite spiritual, with a strong connection to spirit, and would be very good with confidentiality. The large yellow stamen indicates strong boundaries, good inner strength, and a person who copes well with stress and who is honest and reliable.

Gerberas show happy, smiling faces to the world. They look cheerful and are usually chosen by cheerful people. They bring brightness and colour into a room and are really lovely flowers to work with. When you look into the centre, you will sometimes get the feeling of a lot of people or a crowd. This may mean that the person comes from a large family, is a public speaker, or just loves company. The bright, clear colours indicate a sunny personality and someone who looks to the future with hope and anticipation.

Think about your own *favourite flowers*. Mine would include some of the ones mentioned in this book, and many more. A garden is such a delight, and while I am not a good gardener, I love to be in the garden. It is a place where we automatically pick up energy from the plants and trees. I always leave the garden feeling uplifted and appreciative of the wondrous colours and serenity I find there. I remember to thank the garden spirits who work tirelessly to make our garden a haven, helping John—my business partner and an excellent gardener—to bring out the true beauty of the flowers, shrubs, and trees. Our garden has huge crystals that John brought back from Brazil. They lift the energies and promote strong and healthy growth. When walking through our garden, you can feel the energy of the clear quartz, rose quartz, and fluorite. We can connect easier to our spirit guides and teachers in this environment.

Twigs with Leaves

Sometimes you are given a twig to read instead of a flower. This may mean that the person you are reading for was in a hurry or that the twig appealed to them. Notice if the twig is knotty (which shows problems) or smooth. You may get a feeling that the person is rushing through life and not taking time for them.

Are there leaves on the stem? Leaves show growth and new happenings. Dead leaves show that it is time to move on from someone or something.

Are the leaves new green or old green? Bright, spring-green leaves give you the promise of a happy future, while dull-green leaves may indicate a nervous disposition or things moving out of a person's life, leaving them feeling vulnerable.

Case Study #1: Reading a Purple Iris for a Lady

The stem of the iris is very straight and flexible, which indicates a strong personality, a person who has a strong sense of what is right and wrong. This strength would be shared with family, friends, co-workers, and students. The lady with this lovely purple flower would live with integrity and a close connection to her spirit guide and to the angels.

This flower is soft and gentle, showing the compassion and caring nature of this lady. It has a firm support, indicating that the lady is confident in her life or that she has a strong group around her, offering her support and love.

The rich, green leaves show the ability to continually learn and grow; they are broad and solid, representing security and balance.

Deep inside the iris, we find the yellow centre at the heart of the flower. This shows a strong mind and the ability to be mentally strong when needed.

This lady would make a very good friend, as she would be reliable and kind and would be able to keep confidential information to herself. Healing ability would be indicated. The negative here would be that she may do too much for others and have difficulty receiving.

You should be open to spirit for assistance in finding out more about this person.

Case Study #2: Reading Frangipanis for a Man

There are eight heads on the lovely stem of this flower, and they shows happiness and enjoyment in life. An ability to be a public speaker would be indicated. This flower may also show that this person has a lot of children or enjoys the company of little ones. The rich yellow centre shows that he thinks on his feet and is always active and moving around. This person is happy in his own company or in groups, and he may work or spend weekends with lots of people. He is bright and vibrant, with a soft and caring centre, and would make a bright and interesting partner.

The big, broad leaves would show that this person is open to many new things and would like to have some adventures.

The main stem is strong, as are the little ones holding the individual flowers, showing courage and reliability. There may be little nodules on the stems, indicating lessons to be learned or problems the person has already overcome. If there is a short stem without a flower, someone of importance has come and gone from his life. Feel deeply to learn how the person was affected by this and how they moved on from it—or if they are still experiencing loss.

The lovely white and yellow flowers show a connection to spirit and a need to work with honesty and grace. The yellow shows intelligence and confidence. Go deeper within to see what you need to pass on to this person.

Case Study #3: Reading a Bottle Brush for a Lady

You will immediately notice that the stem is thick and solid, with little or no flexibility, giving you a basis to start your reading by suggesting that the lady needs to be a little more flexible with her ideas to find happiness. The bottle brush, although attractive, feels prickly, so she may be sharp—or rough-spoken.

She may be highly critical of others and may have trust issues. This lady may be a fighter who enjoys confrontation and who runs on adrenaline, having no patience with people who are not as intelligent or who take longer to learn things.

Her love life may be in tatters, as she has a problem showing love and affection—although she will buy presents and think this is just as good. This lady may operate from the head instead of the heart, not realizing that she has so many problems. Tact and diplomacy fly out the door when she opens her mouth, and she can walk out of a room not knowing she has left many gobsmacked people in her wake.

You would offer many suggestions to this lady to improve her life: regular massages (to break down some blockages), walks on the beach, going to funny movies, making a friend but dropping the judgment, or doing a reiki class to lift her vibrations or a meditation class to help her still her mind.

When you are reading, remember that everyone thinks they are okay, so you need tact and diplomacy to help her make changes. Listen carefully for any messages from her guide.

The points made here are ideas for you to work from. Flowers hold lots of vibrations from the people who hold them, so they are fairly easy to read. Enjoy reading for family and friends while you are practicing. You will learn different aspects to read from flowers, and I wish you much joy in reading them.

Chapter 21

Reading Ribbon Sticks

Y ou will use ribbons sticks to read a person's emotional body, future, and maybe some options for success. Ribbon sticks are lovely to read. They feel great, and the colours give you a good start with your information.

During this reading, you will run the coloured ribbons through your fingers after they have been held by the person you are reading for. This is again a vibrational reading.

Make yourself some coloured healing and ribbon sticks by buying coloured ribbons in a variety of colours from shops. You also need pieces of dowelling about thirty centimetres long—or some chopsticks—to attach the ribbons to. You will choose about twelve different ribbons for each ribbon stick.

Ribbons are to be different colours and textures, some with patterns and braid and others as smooth as silk. Let the width vary, and have some with fine edges and some with corded edges

Cut your ribbons into pieces about forty-five centimetres long, and stick them to the dowelling with craft glue, giving them plenty of time to dry. Choose a variety of colours and stick the ribbons to the wood in a row. Prepare six sticks for readings, so you have a good variety.

I will offer some suggestions to start your thinking, but once you start, you will get other thoughts, words, and phrases to assist you with your reading. Always remember to be kind with your words and to explain yourself well.

When you are ready to read, ask the person to let the ribbons flow through their fingers a few times, putting their vibrations into them. After two to four minutes, ask the person to close their eyes, pick out three to five ribbons for you to read, and then hand them to you.

It is easier if you flow the unused ribbons down one side of your leg and the ones you are about to read on the other side. Pick up one ribbon at a time to read. Let the ribbon slide through your fingers for a while, letting your thoughts go, and reach out with your mind for pictures and information. Read your ribbons aloud one at a time with compassion and accuracy, being helpful and encouraging at all times.

Below are the meanings for the colours I work with when reading and healing. There are many more options, so work with your colours and record your own thoughts and answers. Spirit will guide you when you connect and are sincere in your endeavours.

Ribbon Colours

Navy or Dark Blue

On the positive side, this person can go to the inner realms and is capable of connecting to spirit to work and promote personal development. They have good meditation skills, and if they aren't using them, maybe you could encourage them to do so. A deep thinker, they would give good advice when asked for it. Excellent at meditation, with the ability to sit quietly in the silence. They do not need to be entertained at all times, as there is a need for quiet times to balance the busy times. It is possible that there is a trip over water, to water, or to another state coming up for them. You may be reading for a philosopher who loves to read and learn.

On the negative side, there may be communication difficulties, or the person may be a good communicator on only one subject, possibly work. They may not be as good at communicating with family or lovers. The enquirer may be a recluse and have speech difficulties, like stammering or shyness or even lack of tact. This colour may at times indicate depression or possibly a problem with bones or teeth. Tact may be needed in a particular situation. It could be that there are signs of reclusive behavior.

Medium and Sky-Blue

This colour could tell you that the person is fun-loving, a chatterbox who enjoys life and is able to make others laugh. Maybe it is someone who can cope very well with unexpected changes and enjoys a challenge. It may take your mind to thinking about water or a journey over water or to clear days ahead and some good times coming. It may indicate an author who has the ability to write courses or poetry. This person could have the ability to be a teacher or public speaker. As good communication skills come with the colour blue, you might like to suggest that the person take a counselling course. Meditation may also be highlighted by this lovely colour, either to write or to enjoy the silence.

On the other hand, we could be encountering emotional problems that need to be solved, problems based on fear or intensiveness. This person may be in a co-dependent relationship and looking for ways to become empowered.

Pale Blue

Travel for work—interstate or overseas—could be coming up. They would be responsible with a light-heartedness that would make them popular. This person would accept life's challenges with grace.

On the negative side it could show a lack of confidence in speaking publicly. There may be an inability to sort out current problems and a need to reach out for help.

Yellow

Optimism and bright, fresh ideas will be coming quickly into this person's life, bringing happiness and lots of laughs, along with happy times with friends and family or a special occasion or holiday. Honesty is highlighted as one of your client's virtues. They are able to set and maintain their own personal boundaries. There may be unexpected gifts coming that will bring joy.

The client you are reading for may also be feeling overly emotional at this time, acting like a victim or a drama queen. They may need to look at how they created this situation and what can be learnt from it.

Mustard

This colour indicates that a healing may just be starting after a serious illness or an emotional time and that this person is reaching out for advice and help. They may find they need to do some releasing work or have a reiki treatment to bring them back into balance.

The mustard colour may also indicate a need to do some liver cleansing and to cut back on additives and sugar while the body repairs some damage.

Pale Yellow

Childlike qualities are indicated here, with a tendency to enjoy playing and laughing like a child and finding joy in the little things in life. This could be a happy person, a nurturer who shows the world a softer face. They may be very good working with children. Children's birthdays, sporting finals, or anniversaries could be coming up in the near future. Good results after exams may be heading their way.

Pale yellow may also indicate a lack of confidence and self-esteem. This person needs encouraging words of approval to lift their energies. They might tell half-truths and lies if they feel inadequate in the workplace or among friends.

Red

Passion, enthusiasm and lots of energy make your client popular and enthusiastic. A happy person who enjoys sex and sensuality and will be in a good relationship or waiting for one to come into their life. They like to explore new ideas, new places, and new cultures.

Busy and competitive, They are usually fairly athletic and most likely fairly strong-willed. In the workplace, ambition and drive will take this person into top positions. If they have recently applied for a new job, they will probably get it. Strong family ties—and possibly strong religious ties—are indicated.

There may be problems with circulation indicated, and issues with the feet or legs may be coming in. They can focus for too long on one thing, needing to let it go and move on in life. They may have an anger problem that needs to be addressed, or be a workaholic and not care about their own health. This colour can bring in the energy of a controller or of an intellectual snob.

Orange

Orange is the colour for inspirational, creative, and artistic ideas. A person choosing orange would have good taste and an eye for colour and style, loving music, texture, and colour. It could be that a female is very fertile and is trying to get pregnant or is in the early stages of pregnancy. A desire for children or to be with children is shown with orange. The person choosing orange may be a good author, actor, or artist. This colour indicates sensuousness and playfulness.

On the other hand, orange can indicate flare-ups of bad sportsmanship, temper tantrums, and jealousy. It can also reveal periodic pain, the inability to get pregnant, or a person who is heavily into pornography. This person may be very materialistic and spend most their time at work. Unhappiness is often indicated.

Green

New friends or lovers will be coming in. Your client may be ready to travel to new and exciting places. A change of residence would be a possibility. New skills will take them into the next period of their life, so they would benefit from taking some new courses. Balance and harmony are coming into their life, and someone will show them empathy and kindness in the near future. There will be opportunities to nurture others or to be nurtured. This person may have healing skills that could be developed and used to help self and others. Healing done by this person would be from the heart.

It is also possible that your client may be feeling a little envious of others at this point in time, or they could be experiencing jealousy that could lead to spitefulness. Unfortunately they may be willing to break up relationships to get who or what they want, or they may be placing too much importance on material things instead of love and affection. There may be a need to move forward into positive thoughts and actions.

Lime

You may be reading for a very uplifting happy soul, who is eager for the next step in life. A new baby or new creative idea is on the way.

Lime would indicate someone who may try to take on the worries of the world and be drained by others. They would give too much of themselves to people who are happy to take and take.

Turquoise

Turquoise is wonderful for healing the inner child and bringing joy and happiness into a person's life. Good fortune may be on the way, and the heart will be open to love where it least expects to find it. This lovely colour attracts wealth and good fortune, and it heals the physical body, especially the immune system.

A person like this may need power and control over others or may have deep-seated depression and childish or selfish behaviour.

Pink

This colour indicates heartfelt love with gentleness and kindness toward self and others. Compassion and empathy are highlighted, along with a love of children and self-nurturing. Unconditional love surrounds the person you are reading for, and they also send out the same love and warmth to others. New love might be on the way—or a reunion with a loved one.

Weight disorders and loneliness may be problems with the negative pink. Bereavement may be ruling this person's life with a sadness that will not abate. Bad, childlike behaviour may also be indicated.

Purple

Purple is a deeply spiritual colour. This colour connects the person to their guides and angels and helps them to tap into the collective mind. This indicates someone who would be open to messages and inspiration and would be prepared to look deeply into their purpose. They may enjoy meditation or prayer. This may herald a time for big changes in the person's life.

This person may also preach to others and be very locked into limited thinking. Tunnel vision may hold back positive progress.

White

People choosing white have a need to nurture others. They are open to blessings and help from their spirit guides and live in a state of grace. If they have too much solitude, they may lose some social skills. They can be perfectionists who are critical of others.

Indigo

It may be time for the enquirer to turn knowledge into wisdom and to use the skills of clairvoyance, clairaudience, and clairsentience. Activating the third eye chakra would improve esoteric skills. Mood swings and hot flushes can make life uncomfortable. Severe headaches may be a problem.

Lavender

Lavender brings in a feeling of peacefulness, softness, and serenity. Feminine healing may be needed. This person may feel disenchanted and disconnected or may lapse into the "why-me" syndrome.

Gold

A win may be coming bringing—success, attainment, or contentment. Good health is indicated and a strength of character. You would be reading for a person who cares for others who are less fortunate. Public recognition could be coming their way. Greed may also be indicated.

Silver

Silver brings in a smooth road ahead, and all problems will be solved with intuition and tact. Nurturing is required, as this person may be running on empty, feeling unable to cope, or feeling unconnected to the source.

Magenta

This would indicate a lovely, warm-hearted person who looks after others. The person you are reading for would be caring, affectionate and generous with their time and energies. They may have an extended family. Positive happenings could be coming.

However, this person may not be spending enough time alone. They may be far too busy looking after others, which would indicate a need for personal nurturing and time alone in silence.

Ribbon Textures and Other Qualities

If a ribbon is *smooth*, the pathway in front of the enquirer is smooth. They may be coming out of a rough patch, with better times ahead with good times coming. We could also read a good trip ahead or success with a venture.

Wide ribbons indicate lots of emotions, and it may be time for the enquirer to be flexible in accepting lots of ideas. This person may need to build their confidence and possibly study for self-improvement or a new career. Lots of choices are open to them at this time.

A *narrow* ribbon indicates that a person may be faced with uncertainty—possibly the end of a venture—or they could have a narrow view of the future.

When a ribbon has *rough edges*, it is possible that a person's problems can be easily resolved and that their life will be improved. A *heavy border* pattern may mean continuous difficulties, unless the person changes certain ideas or pathways.

Smooth edges make a person's pathway easier to traverse.

A ribbon with *heavy patterns* indicates that a person will experience lots of twists, turns, and obstacles along the way. It is time to pay attention to detail. *Light patterns* indicate that minor obstacles are coming to be dealt with but that the person is nearly there in their thinking.

Beading on the ribbon indicates someone who loves life and who is currently experiencing—and will go on to experience—fun, joy, and happiness. Minor obstacles will be easily overcome.

If *stars* are on the ribbon, good luck is on the way—especially if the person is seeking a better future. A windfall is likely in this lifetime to help this person's journey. Stars may also indicate a person with childlike behaviour, looking for attention.

Doing the Reading

Issues you feel on first touching the ribbon would include day-to-day matters and current problems, possible highlights for the future, and possibly the names of incoming people. You may feel light-hearted when you touch the ribbon—or happy or sad or full of expectation for the future. Work with your clairvoyance and clairsentience to see if you can form mind pictures to go with your feelings. Start talking about the thoughts you are having and take the time to go within to find answers. Do not rush yourself. It is better to be slow and accurate.

Does the ribbon run smoothly through your fingers? Does the way ahead appear to be free-flowing, or do you falter as you run your fingers through the ribbon? Do you get stuck, knowing that you have found some difficulties?

If you get names or places, give them to the person, as they may mean something now or further along their life's pathway.

Remember that there is no need to be dramatic. You do not need to shock or scare people. Your job at all times is to help, to make suggestions and then let the details go, as you aren't entitled to walk people's lives with them. Aim to build confidence and self-esteem, and give them any tools you think may be of service to them.

Example #1

Imagine that you are reading three ribbons for a lady: a wide, yellow, smooth ribbon with a thicker edge; a thin, white ribbon; and a peach-coloured, medium ribbon.

Start by running the yellow ribbon through your hands. Considering the width and sunny aspect of the yellow, you may feel that this lady has good confidence and self-esteem and is mainly a joyful and happy person. You might feel a certain amount of stress (the yellow being the colour of the solar plexus chakra, which is the centre for stress), and in your mind you would be looking for pictures of the reason for this stress. You are trying to feel whether the stress is a problem or if the lady uses stress to motivate herself.

You would feel that she is honest and has good boundaries. She has the ability to say no and to stand her ground in a confrontation.

You would also search in your intuition for problems with the stomach or digestive area.

Moving on to the white ribbon, you may feel that the lady has started her spiritual journey and is seeking more answers. She works with her conscience and gut feelings to help others and to keep herself on track. She may be looking for a teacher or a spiritual group to join for help and support.

The peach ribbon would indicate new inspiration and excitement over a new project that may only be just beginning. This colour represents artistry, so the lady may be a writer, painter, interior decorator, or something similar. She would have very good taste and a good sense of colour. Another possibility here is that she may be pregnant, soon-to-be pregnant, or about to learn of a pregnancy near to her.

There are many ways to read this colourful combination, and these suggestions should start you with your readings.

Example #2

Now we will read a medium-blue ribbon, a red ribbon, and a gold ribbon for a man.

Starting with the blue ribbon, your thoughts may go toward him being a good communicator or someone who communicates for work, e.g., a reporter, author, commentator, teacher, or lecturer. Maybe he is just someone with a good gift for languages. The blue colour could indicate a trip over water—or that his emotions are running high with things he has not had the opportunity to say. Remember your clairsentience—what are you feeling right now about this blue ribbon. Is it slipping easily through your fingers, or is it getting stuck, indicating problems? This man could also be facing an important choice in his life and feeling unsure of how to handle the challenges involved.

The red ribbon indicates ambition and drive, the ability to forge forward when necessary. This person will be energetic and forceful at times and a go-getter in his employment. He has the energy and conviction of his ideas to do very well in life. He may need to watch that he doesn't step on others along the way or forget to give his family the attention they deserve.

The gold ribbon indicates success, reaching a goal, and getting rewarded. A promotion may be on the way. There is also a certain amount of cleansing to be done—either physical or emotional—for this to happen.

CHAPTER 22

Reading Feathers

When reading a feather, we are looking at the entire life of the client. Starting at the base of the feather, we look at the tender years, the teenage years, adulthood, maturity, and senior years.

To do this reading, we need to use our intuition. Take note of the colour or colours of the feather. Look at the spine: is it strong, rigid, or flexible? Look for breaks in the feather where life might have been on-hold for a while. Ask yourself if the feather feels rough or smooth. Use your clairsentience. What are you feeling while you are holding this feather?

Hold the feather in your hand and feel the vibrations of the person you are reading for.

The base of the feather shows childhood. Moving through the person's life as you make your way up the spine of the feather. Check the length before you start and estimate in your head the approximate ages as you work the feather.

Colour of the Feather

Look at the colour of the feather and think about what it means to you.

If the feather is *black*, this person may have experienced loneliness and separation at some stage in this lifetime. They may also have suffered depression and/or abandonment. They would have great inner strength and, through introspection, would have learned many lessons to advance their journey. This person would be a deep thinker who could work on their own and possibly meditate to connect to spirit. If they haven't worked through their issues, they may have anger management problems or have difficulty finding love.

As you can see, there are many positive and negative thoughts that can come into your mind, so the clairsentience is very important. You need to feel which answers call to you and then add your own thoughts.

A *grey* feather may indicate someone who tries hard to get it right and may still be waiting for the good times. This person would be a good listener and could at times be indecisive. They may make lots of plans but hesitant in seeing things through to the finish. Some people who choose grey live their lives through their children. They can be dreamers who like their own space and can get stuck in the small details.

A person who chooses a *white* feather has a strong connection to spirit and a true desire to help others. This person is light-hearted and joyful, and enjoys the company of others. They are fun to be with, mix well with groups, and can laugh at themselves. Honesty is important to this person. They work hard and often live in a state of grace.

A *brown* feather would indicate a person who is grounded and practical in thinking. They would be stable and would appreciate security and their own home. Very responsible in the work area and at home, they make good friends and partners. Also they can be a little bit slow in making decisions.

A *green* feather shows a balanced personality, a person who is caring and sharing. This person may be a care worker, nurse, or counsellor and would be a good, complimentary healer. Harmony is important to them and their home would reflect this. This person would love spending time with nature.

The person who chooses a *blue* feather would be a good communicator and a good healer. They would enjoy challenges. They would walk their own pathway through life with lots of tact and diplomacy and would be an engaging person to spend time with. This person would have lots of choices to make in this lifetime, many of vital importance.

A *speckled* feather indicates a varied life with lots of changes of jobs and house moves. This person would be rather restless and may have many lovers and friends. There is a tendency to be light-hearted, with the possibility of being irresponsible at times. Basically, this is a fun person who likes variety and lots of fun.

A feather that is *black with blue or green* may indicate a deep thinker with healing abilities. The person may have patches of brilliance in the area of career, but may also suffer with depression at times. They would be happiest with a well-balanced partner.

Texture of the Feather

A *smooth and tidy* feather indicates a more orderly life or personality that can cope with the tough patches.

A *rough and scruffy* feather shows that a lot of grit and determination will be needed in this lifetime, as the person has taken on some heavy challenges.

A *spiky* feather indicates that you are reading for a touchy person who does not suffer fools gladly. This person lacks tact at times, being brittle and hard in their opinions. They speak sharply and may suffer with throat problems.

A *smooth* feather may demonstrate abundance in either finances or emotional stability. It indicates that this person is taking an easier path through life.

A *battered and squashed* feather may be indicative of obsessive and compulsive behaviours, addiction, and a huge lack of confidence. This person would need kind words—and maybe some counselling—to help them get back on track. You would expect this person to have had a troubled childhood and to be in need of love.

When *chunks are missing* from the feather, this may show that bereavement, divorce, or separation has had a huge impact on this person. They may also have experienced a serious illness. Bankruptcy may also feature here.

Spine of the Feather

If the feather's spine is *strong*, this person has the mental fortitude to survive difficult times and has an assertive nature with which they will find their own solutions to problems. They may become a leader in their field of expertise.

A *flexible* spine indicates an able person who can go with the flow and change direction in life if necessary. They will get on well with others, being kind-hearted and eager to please.

The person presenting a *weak, soft, or bent* feather would be easily swayed by others and unable to give strong opinions of their own.

The owner of an *unyielding* feather would be unable to change the course of their life due to stubbornness. They would be hard to live with, possibly being a controller at home and in the work place. This person would have a need to always be right.

Assessing the Feather

Look at the feather and let your thoughts form around the qualities you observe.

Is it strong? Is it soft? Is it a combination of both? Is it smooth? How does this make you feel? Are there pieces missing? What does this mean to you?

What age do you think the missing pieces point to? What do you think was happening at that time in the person's life? Run your hand over the feather. What do you see? What are you feeling in your heart when you hold this feather? What are you hearing from spirit? Do you feel a beautiful spirit or a troubled one?

Reading a feather opens doorways in your mind to access the person at different times in their life, giving them an opportunity to clear old baggage, remember the good times, and move forward with ease. You will be able to comment on many things that have occurred in this person's life and, hopefully, give them some interesting ideas for the future.

Example #1

This feather is to be read for a man. It is black from the base to three quarters of the way up the spine, finishing with grey. It is scruffy at the bottom, with gaps along the spine. The spine is rough with little flexibility most of the way to the top. The top is tidy and together.

This feather would reveal a strong soul with the determination to push through adversity. An unhappy childhood is indicated for this person, maybe with a dominating parent and or lack of money and security. He may have experienced domestic violence or witnessed his mother as the victim. He would have had to learn to keep his opinions and thoughts to himself to prevent being in trouble.

Bullying would also be indicated here, so talk to him about his life at school, which may have been difficult for several reasons. He may have been weak and picked-on, a rebel who did not conform, or a student who lacked appropriate clothing or clean schoolbooks or a space or time at home to do homework. He may have experienced many sad and lonely years, feeling inadequate and lost.

He may have left these years behind him but carried a chip on his shoulder for many years, possibly resenting those who had it easy.

The positive outcome of these tough times and lonely years would be the ability to keep his own counsel, strength, and courage.

Running your eyes up the feather, you find that bits are missing. During these times, the person has experienced loneliness and has struggled with his emotions. He may be coping with a broken marriage or relationship, bereavement, or loss of a good job. Sad times are indicated, so look to see how often this has occurred.

There is a feeling that the person may not be very flexible in his thinking, as security will be important to him. He may tend to be driven and very focused, not allowing for fun and relaxation.

Moving further up the feather, we find the grey starting to come in and a smoother feel to the feather.

You feel that, at this point, his life improved. Maybe someone came along to love him, or maybe he did a lot of work on himself and to cope with life and all of its challenges.

Look intuitively for the right answers here. How are you feeling, now that you have headed into easier energy?

You can now encourage this person by explaining that life will improve and happiness will be there for him. Advise him to stay positive, to be open to new people and places, and to find an inner peace.

Example #2

Now we will do a sample reading for a lady, using a small, white, fluffy feather.

This cute feather gives a light vibration. You feel a childhood filled with loving people, happy Christmases, and hunts for Easter eggs. The feeling here is lovely and inspiring. It makes you think of joy and happiness, laughter and children playing. This feeling may indicate that the lady works with children or enjoys her own. A loving family springs to mind, with stable relationships and support. You feel that the person who brought this feather is very happy and content with her life. The fluffiness shows her sense of humour and childlike view of the world. You feel that this person is protected, but she is in fact capable of looking after herself. All the way up the feather, the feelings remain the same, so a very balanced life is indicated. The white could indicate that this person is connected to spirit and may work in the spiritual healing or teaching fields.

When people bring feathers to you to read, it is amazing how accurate you can be, as the feathers they choose will always reflect their lives. You can be of service by giving them encouragement and helpful advice.

Chapter 23

Reading Sand

ou will need a tray filled with clean, white sand. Sift the sand to make sure it is perfectly clean.

Ask your client to sit quietly and place their hands in the sand, palms downward, allowing their vibrations to go into the sand and give you information to read. Wait quietly for a few minutes.

Then take the client's place and put your hands lightly onto their fingerprints in the sand. Close your eyes and clear your mind as you wait for pictures and thoughts. Think about what this information means to you, and discuss this information with the person you are reading for.

Ask yourself some questions. Where does this person live? Are they married? Do they have children? What is this person's favourite thing to do? Do they like music? What is their favourite colour? More questions will come into your head as you start to get answers. Stay focused and stay positive as you read.

Case Study #1

This reading was done for a lady in her fifties. Anna lives in the beautiful city of Adelaide, the capital of South Australia. This is part of her reading.

I saw Anna as a child, sitting in the dirt, playing with cars, making roads and hills, and humming to herself. I had the feeling I was in the arid Australian outback, and this was confirmed.

She felt very happy and content at this time. Her life was simple, her parents were loving, and her days were filled with adventures. During this time, she acquired a love of the great outback—the smells, the sounds, and the continuous flow of visitors who wandered in from the road to the station she lived on.

"Were you happy as a child?" I asked her. "Were you very close to your parents in your early years?" I felt such joy and happiness from her at this time of her life. She replied that she was very happy as a child in the Australian outback.

I moved my mind forward a few years to a wedding day filled with love, laughter, and smiles. She was extremely happy to marry the man she adored. Anna confirmed that it was her perfect day, and they had been very much in love.

I moved forward to the birth of several children, each one special in its own way and each bringing great happiness and joy into her life. I felt again the love and contentment in Anna's life.

Moving forward again, I felt that I was standing at a child's funeral. The energy was heavy and very sad, and I felt resentment and great pain and suffering emanating from Anna. I felt that the child had passed over after an accident and that Anna blamed her husband for this loss. Anna confirmed that this was so. A bleak period in her life followed, as she and her husband started to go their own ways. The remaining children lived in a less than happy home, and when they were old enough, they left home.

I felt Anna spiral down into depression and inner pain. I experienced her sadness when her husband left to start a new life with a different lady. I felt that Anna hadn't wanted him to go but couldn't find the words she needed to ask him to stay.

Moving forward again, I saw Anna move to Adelaide and make a new friend who would bring some laughter back into her life. I could see her going out shopping and laughing over coffee.

It seemed to me that I had caught up with the current period in Anna's life. I reached into the future and saw Anna going out with a couple of men. Then I saw one very important man come into her life. He was a man who, like Anna, had a love of the Australian outback, who liked to travel, and who had lots of energy for new adventures.

Going further into her future, I saw them marry in a garden with her children around her, and I saw the Pacific Islands as their honeymoon destination.

I stopped the reading here, feeling that this lovely lady had many years of happiness ahead of her and that gradually her sadness would fade.

I concluded the reading by giving her messages from her son in spirit. He came in to tell her to be happy and to let her know that he was safe and content in spirit.

Do you always get this much from a sand reading? No, you don't. What came through on that day was the help Anna needed to move forward.

Case Study #2

This was a sand reading for an elderly gentleman.

Putting my hands into the sand, I felt great sorrow, and I knew it was because of the death of his long-time wife. Their marriage had been wonderful, and they had found much joy in each other's company. I thought about the little things that she had said to him, and he responded that it was so.

I looked ahead to a time when he would have a lady companion but not a lover or a wife. I felt that he was still on this earth to be of service to others. I could see him doing reiki in the future, talking to others about death and dying, and giving them strength. I felt the pride his wife would feel when he was so kind and understanding to others. I didn't feel that he would ever get over the death of his lovely wife, but the time would come when he would be busier and not so heartbroken. These two people were a match made in heaven, and one day he will return to the love of his life.

Case Study #3

This reading was for a lady in her mid-thirties.

I saw a new home with a wide lawn and a lovely garden. The home was big and the rooms were large. Two little girls were playing on the lawn, throwing a ball back and forth as I watched them.

I could see a dark-haired man weeding the garden, and I had the impression that it was a job he didn't like. He was, however, enjoying watching his children play in the sunshine. I felt that the home was filled with love and happiness. (After the reading, the lady phoned me when she reached home and validated everything I had seen: her husband and daughters were still in the garden of their fairly new home. She told me that her husband hated weeding but couldn't stand still, so he had to do something while watching the girls).

At this point in the reading, we were joined by a spirit woman in her twenties who had passed in a car accident. It was a friend who was sorely missed, and she had the opportunity to pass on messages of reassurance and love to the client. This was a short reading, but everything was validated, and happiness radiated from it.

CHAPTER 24

Reading Photographs

Keep your notebook handy, and write down your impressions. In your hands, hold a photograph with the image facing away from you, and see what you feel before you look at the photograph. Work out if you are reading for a man or a woman. See if you can intuitively get an age for the person and whether they were happy at the time the picture was taken. Reach out with your mind. Do you have thoughts, feelings, or mind pictures of a family, career, hobbies, favourite movie, sport, or artistic persuits? Do you think this person is in a committed relationship?

Now turn the photograph over and look at the person. Can you make contact with their eyes? How have your impressions changed? What can you tell from looking at the face? Future predictions for them may include wonderful happenings, special occasions, or ways of empowering themselves.

Case Study #1

I read a photo of a lady who had passed on. She looked about seventy in the photo, and she was wearing a lovely knitted Fair Isle cardigan. As we linked, she immediately told me that she had made it.

I had the impression that she did a lot of knitting for her family, but she was bit annoyed that they didn't always appreciate or wear her lovely garments. I asked her to validate this and found it to be true. The granddaughters found her cardigans a bit too old-fashioned for today's world. I felt that she was a good cook, especially with pastry and scones, but didn't like to bake cakes or fiddly things. The lady validated this and said she didn't like to ice cakes or make intricate desserts. She was a little short of patience and found that being old was a jolly nuisance. She loved her family and was happy in spirit with her husband, who had passed many years before her.

She told me where to find some of her jewellery, which apparently went missing as soon as she died. The person who had taken it did not get any pleasure from it, as she couldn't wear it without being seen and caught. This tickled the old lady, who said that this person should never have taken it in the first place.

She commented on her son-in-law and the fact that they didn't really get along. She thought he should move right along, away from her daughter, as he was very bossy and controlling.

I found this lady to be entertaining and really quite witty. I think she would have been a no-nonsense person when she was on earth with her family. The family was thrilled to hear from her—although perhaps a little startled by her pithy comments.

Case Study #2

When I was reading a photograph of a young child, I started with the photograph facing away from me so I couldn't see the picture, and I had a feeling of asthma or breathing difficulties. My own breathing became laboured and shallow. I thought this would be a child who didn't go outside to play very much. Possibly she was a bit smothered with love and was a little delicate. When I turned the photograph over, I saw that the little girl was lovely, with sweet smile and a happy face. I had the feeling that, given the opportunity, she would have improved her health with some outdoor time and a family holiday where she could play with other children. The mother was not open to this suggestion, saying that she did keep the little one inside most of the time.

I saw the girl playing the piano and having classes in her own home. When she got older, a new friend would come into her life like a breath of fresh air. There would be a big improvement in her health, and her mother would hold less power over her. I thought that this would cause a lot of trouble at home, and I hoped that the mother would find new interests and not need to play on her daughter's health for control. I had the impression of happiness and romance in her twenties. At this time in her life, she would experience freedom and some travel to open up her world. I encouraged the mother to go out more and to make some friends, as her own life was also very restricted by her limiting thought patterns. I handed the photo back with a slightly heavy heart, knowing it would be years before the changes started.

Case Study #3

I was handed a baby's photo to read and immediately realized that the baby was in spirit. I really like to read photos of people who are still on this plane, but sometimes people need closure, and it is my job as a reader to give that, if possible.

The parents thought that they were being punished in some way by losing this beautiful child.

I felt that this simply wasn't so. I felt the need to look into a past life that was applicable to the current life to find some answers. My guide suggested that the parents had elected to lose a child as part of their development. They had made this decision because of their actions in a past life where they had been responsible for many abortions. This had been their own choice, and they found the lesson difficult. In their sadness, the parents had decided not to have any more children, fearing that it would happen again. The message from their child was full of love and encouragement, and it also told them of two children yet to come and much joy in the years ahead.

Is this always the case when you lose a child? Certainly not. The reasons and decision to lose a child are one's own, but they are usually associated with accelerated growth, building empathy and compassion in one's chakras. It is a very difficult decision to make, and I truly respect those who walk this road. Some of the best parents on earth lose a child. They may be good people who made this the decision for their own growth, or maybe the child just needed a few years on earth before going back to get ready for the next incarnation. We can never judge a decision made by another person, as we do not know the karma behind that decision.

All children are precious gifts from spirit. The joy of carrying the child of the partner you love—right under your heart chakra—is indescribable. I consider myself to be extremely lucky to have two lovely children who have enriched my life.

Children are part of your soul's contract. You promise in spirit to love and cherish them, to educate them, and to empower them so they may have a good start to their lives.

My guides tell me that they consider thirty to be the age of maturity, not eighteen or twenty-one.

CHAPTER 25

Reading Coloured Fabric

Obtain a box of coloured fabric squares, about eight centimetres on a side. Ask a person to choose seven coloured squares from a large variety of different colours with their eyes closed and then place them in a vertical line, starting at the bottom and moving upward.

Each square will represent a chakra, with the bottom square being the base chakra.

Work with your knowledge of chakras and colours to do this reading. You may like to refer to the colours in the chapter about reading flowers. There are many good books on chakras for you to read. I am listing only a small amount of information for each chakra to get you started. It would be wise to read as many books as possible on chakras and to use this information in readings and in healing sessions.

You may at times find that the person you are reading for will choose the actual chakra colour. Other times it may be very different. Just read what you find. Let the words and thoughts come into your head, and ask your spirit guide to be close to you and to help you with your reading. When referring to the chosen colour, feel what it means to you and what it means to your client. I have included many questions for you to consider when working with the chakras.

Base Chakra (Red)

Your base chakra refers to your upbringing and home life, vitality, education, and religious beliefs.

Touching the fabric the client has chosen, ask yourself questions. How safe did this person feel as a child? How much love was in their life? How strict was their upbringing? What old hurts are they carrying that need to be released? Are they in a safe and comfortable environment now? How much energy do they have to go about their daily life? Is gratitude or resentment the main energy in their life? Are they motivated, full of vitality, and enthusiastic about their life? Are they reaching for their full potential? Do you feel that they will be secure in the future? What suggestions can you make to help them build a better future? Consider the clients relationship with parents, siblings, and friends, and comment on how they relate to others. Do you feel that they have ambition and drive? Is success and achievement heading their way?

Sacral Chakra (Orange)

This chakra looks at sexuality and sensuality. You may feel that the enquirer is free to have fun and to be themselves or that they possibly have some fears in the area of sexuality. Do you sense creative energy? Do you have a feeling of good taste, artistic endeavours, or maybe a need to be financially secure? Filled with ambition they may be very material in their outlook, and money may be a driving force in their life. Do they build relationships from the chakra? How do they feel about relationships with partners? Are they looking for love, or do they have a different agenda? What do you see for them in the future? Will they be successful in one of the artistic fields or in love and romance? Do you feel they will have what it takes to go from strength to strength? You may be reading for an artist, author, or singer. What is your general feeling about this person's gifts in this lifetime? Are they attracting success? How does this person relate to co-workers and bosses?

Solar Plexus Chakra (Yellow)

What view does your client hold for themselves? Is the client confident? Is anyone stepping over his or her personal boundaries? Are they stifled or free-spirited? Are they insecure and unable to cope with everyday life? How much time do they spend on appearance? Do you feel that they are honest with themselves and others? Are they able to speak up when necessary and hold firm to their own convictions? How psychic do you think they are? Are they working on improving their talent? Is the person committed to their life and journey? Do they seem to be responsible and capable of looking after themselves? How strong is their need for approval, and is this holding the person back from advancing spiritually? What do they desire, and how are they going about achieving it? What do they do for a living? Do you feel the presence of friends and happy times around? What do you see ahead for them? What can you say to raise their confidence and self-esteem? Does this person reach out for opportunities?

Heart Chakra (Green)

Do the colours green, pink, peach, and red here represent love and passion to you? How do you feel about cool colours like blue, aqua, and white in this position? How loving do you think this person is? How loved do you think they are? Do you get a feeling of kindness and compassion? Do you feel that they have a partner and that they are happy with their life? Do you sense loneliness and a deep wish for a loving relationship? Have they been hurt in the past? Can you see engagements, weddings, and anniversaries in the future? Do they feel fulfilled? Who do they need to forgive? Do you feel that they are blocking their heart because of past hurts? Is this person open to helping others? Ask them, on a scale of one to ten, how much love they send out. When you have the answer, ask, on a scale one to ten, how much love they receive. Work from the answers you receive.

Throat Chakra (Blue)

This is the centre of communication. Are you reading for a good or poor communicator? How can you help them if there is a problem? Are they good at making choices and sticking to them? Do you sense a softening of words when necessary, or are they inclined to be tactless?

Brow Chakra (Indigo)

This is the chakra for our intuitive skills, including clairvoyance, clairsentience, clairaudience, and knowing. How open is the person to these abilities, and how interested do they seem in moving into these energies? Are they dedicated to getting it right? Is honesty part of their journey?

Crown Chakra (White or Violet)

This chakra connects us to everyone in the universe. It gives us basic love toward others and an understanding that life is eternal and that we are still connected to our loved ones who have passed over. We have wonderful, spiritual teachers who work tirelessly for humanity, and we give thanks and appreciation through prayer and meditation. At this chakra, we realize that we are all one.

As you work your way through these chakras and colours, a pattern will emerge, giving you the opportunity to bring up many issues that need to be cleared and to remind the client of special talents and skills they have but may not be using yet. Be kind with your reading, and make it a special and helpful experience.

CHAPTER 26

Reading a Crystal

rystals have wonderful healing energy and are a delight to read. There are several ways to read crystals.

Method #1

Encourage the client to choose a crystal from a bowl and hold it for a while, enmeshing their own vibrations with those of the crystal. When you take the crystal into your hand, read from your feelings, thoughts, and the images being presented to you.

Method #2

Produce a bag of coloured crystals, and ask your client to choose seven of them. After the client holds them for a while, ask them to place the crystals on the table in a vertical line, from bottom to top.

You will read them from the bottom, with each crystal representing a chakra. Commence with the base chakra, the bottom crystal.

The bottom chakra refers to home and family. Do you feel that this person had a happy childhood? Does the person have a happy home now?

The second chakra refers to competition, finance, and how the person relates to others.

159

The third chakra refers to the person's thoughts about themselves—how much self worth they have, and their level of self-esteem.

The fourth chakra refers to matters of the heart and how much love a person has in their heart for themselves and for others.

The fifth chakra refers to a person's communication skills and their ability to speak well and with clarity and tact.

The sixth chakra refers to a person's intuition and psychic abilities. It involves being able to accept spirit messages that have no reason or physical proof.

The seventh chakra refers to a person's connection to the divine and to all of humanity.

Remember to read the chakra and qualities of the crystals together for method number two.

Crystals

Here are some of the crystals you will place in your bag for your client to choose from.

The *amethyst* suggests the need for meditation, relaxation, calmness, and time out to rest and recharge your batteries. It is a lovely crystal to promote spiritual insights.

The *aquamarine* calms and soothes. This crystal is soft and gentle, and it helps you to find clarity as you look inward for your answers.

The *blue topaz* helps you to develop listening skills and to deal with your lessons with truth and honesty.

The *carnelian* helps you to manifest your dreams and to become a co-creator in the universe. It is empowering, promoting creativity and fun times.

Citrine helps you to manifest abundance on all levels—good health, more wealth, and lots of happiness. It clears negativity from your auric field and teaches you to respect yourself.

Diamonds enhance inner visions and connect you to spirit, increasing clarity and awareness of other realms.

The *emerald* is the stone of prosperity, the gemstone that opens the heart chakra, encouraging devotion, compassion, and tenderness.

Fluorite brings clarity in all situations and opens the brow chakra to insights and deeper understanding.

The warm colours and vibrations emanating from *garnets* enhance vitality and warmth and ask you to be true to yourself and trustworthy with others.

Green tourmaline strengthens heart energy, helps you to overcome fears, and promotes spiritual growth.

Jade balances the yin and yang energies and is soothing and calming.

Grounding, centring, calming *jasper* helps to dissolve negativity and strengthens your willpower.

Lapis lazuli brings spiritual enlightenment and improved awareness, and it helps you to connect with your totality.

Opal encourages creativity, strengthens your memory, and builds loyalty.

Malachite dissolves physical pain if worn for several hours. It also eases heartache and helps you to let go of old habits and to release past lives and resentment.

Peridot helps you to cope with change. It may also help you to find new love and new friendship. It is helpful to those who are studying.

Clear quartz amplifies energy, improves memory, aids meditation, and can be programmed to help you to study, improving your recall of facts.

Rose quartz is the stone of love and friendship. It can tell of a new partner coming or a current love becoming more important. It also cools tempers and helps you to find a peaceful solution to your problems.

Safe travel is highlighted with *moonstone*. It also promotes intuitive insight and opens you to a new awareness.

The deep and steadfast love of the *ruby* helps you to create your heart's desire, living your life with optimism and personal courage.

The lovely *blue sapphire* promotes intuitive and psychic abilities, helping you to connect to your inner teacher. It helps with astral travel.

The sunny *yellow sapphire* helps to strengthen the mental body and brings visions and clarity and often financial abundance.

Known widely for its healing abilities, the *turquoise* is very grounding. It helps you to express yourself and improves your communication skills, including the ability to listen.

Case Study

This was a reading for a young woman called Serena, who chose her seven crystals and arranged them in a line on the table.

The bottom crystal was malachite, and this related to her base chakra. Malachite is a dark-green gemstone with black markings, and it is found around Burra in South Australia. This indicated to me that Serena had to let go of a lot of her old, limiting thought patterns. There was pain connected to her family life, and she had a need to reassess the direction she wished to go.

I felt that Serena had been brought up in a family with very strict values and that she had often felt stifled when she wanted to make her own decisions. I recognized an underlying ambition that had helped her to break away from the family for a while to study and find her pathway in life. I felt that the family still put a lot of pressure on her to conform with their rigid ideas. I also had the sense that they wished her to marry and have children, as they thought it was improper for her to still be single in her thirties and living alone.

We worked through some exercises to help her let go of the expectations of others and to empower herself. We also released some of the family traditions, which no longer served her.

Her second choice was a carnelian, an orange/brown colour, for the sacral chakra. This choice showed that she had great vitality and a good sense of humour, and these two traits had helped her to start her new life. She was a sexual and sensual person looking for love and affection in her life. I felt that a couple of romances had come and gone from her life and that she was now ready for someone new to come in. It appeared to me that she was a little overpowering in a relationship and needed to express her needs and ideas in a gentle way. I felt that financially she was secure and was probably buying a home or unit, which she confirmed.

This chakra was strong, and she was on track to a good relationship in the future. I felt that Serena could manifest whatever she wanted in life.

Serena's third choice for the solar plexus chakra was a golden citrine. Citrines have the ability to self clean and to clear negativity from one's aura and physical body.

This is the gemstone for joy, optimism, laughter, and happy times. I saw Serena having wonderful times with friends, curling up in a chair and watching television with an absence of stress. I knew that this lovely lady had spent a lot of time improving herself, lifting her self-esteem and confidence, and that she was proud of the progress she had made so far. I felt her connection to the universe, and I thought that she had a good appreciation of life.

Her choice for the heart chakra was an emerald, the stone for prosperity and deep commitment. This told me that Serena was ready for a strong and deep love with an equal partner who would share her journey, encourage her, and support her emotionally. She was looking for integrity, truth, and compassion and would attract a partner with these qualities, as she possessed them herself. The law of the universe is "like attracts like."

From a difficult home life, this young lady had grown in spiritual strength and wisdom and was forging ahead into a much better life.

We moved next to the gemstone Serena had selected for the throat chakra. Her choice this time was fluorite, with the subtle colours of purple and green.

At the throat chakra, this wonderful stone opens you to a deeper understanding of your life—and the life of all humanity. It gives you clarity in all of your future decisions. It teaches you to think before you speak and to speak with clarity and tactfulness. It encourages you to listen well and to avoid making impulsive decisions. Serena would make many new choices in her life, facing her worries with strength and contemplation.

The stone she chose for the brow chakra was the lapis lazuli, deep-blue with golden flecks glistening in the sunlight. Again, this was a wonderful choice as it would open Serena to spiritual enlightenment. Her awareness would expand, and she would be excited by the potential she has in the spiritual field. I think that she will attend classes to improve her spiritual development and will fly like an eagle with her studies. She expressed interest in learning how to meditate and open her intuition.

The choice for the crown chakra was the clear quartz, which opens and expands the energy and stimulates the mental body. The energy is amplified, so her memory will improve and she will enjoy her studies. I suggested to her that she should include her family at night in her prayers and blessings and simply accept that her way of life is different from theirs. This should not stop the love or the prayers flowing between them all. It appeared that Serena had a wonderful future ahead of her. I think that I saw her at a time when she had worked her way through many difficult issues and was now on track for a brilliant future.

I believe that working with crystals enhances your own energy and ability to find answers to questions. They raise your intuitive powers and psychic abilities. They are also excellent for healing work and are wonderful for gifts. When choosing a crystal for a friend, just think about the person, and you will find your way to the correct crystal for that friend at that time, one that will help with his or her current lesson.

CHAPTER 27

Reading a Shell

Shells are lovely to read. They are connected to our emotional bodies and give a lot of information. They are lovely to hold, and they make excellent jewellery and great adornments for offices or rooms.

Continually cleansed by the ocean, they help us to cleanse our emotions. Ask your client to hold the shell for a while so that it absorbs the emotions and gives you a clear reading. It is always interesting to see which shell a person has brought to be read, as it tells a lot about them.

Closed shells indicate a need for protecting oneself, feeling unsure and maybe a little lost in one's world. Fears may predominate in some lives.

Here are some of the shells you will read.

The calming *abalone* shell settles you when you are being hypersensitive. It collects scattered thoughts and helps you to find clarity. It will aid with self-expression and public speaking.

Mother-of-pearl is a soft, loving, and nurturing energy that brings the gifts of healing and intuition. Compassion is highlighted when you wear mother-of-pearl.

Paua shells remind us that hidden under all of our blockages is a spiritual being having an earth life. Every shell is different to remind us that we are unique spiral beings with many hidden talents and skills.

Reading a Shell

Place a collection of shells in a bowl and ask your client to hold the shell of their choice for a few minutes. Take the shell in your own hands and hold it for a while. Let the feelings come to you. How do you feel holding this shell? Are you happy, sad, balanced, or uneasy? Do you feel stressed? Do you feel that this shell was handed to you by someone who is relaxed and peaceful? As you are asking yourself some of these questions, how does your body feel? Is it reacting? Do you feel tightness in your solar plexus? Are you experiencing tightness or heaviness in your heart? Do you feel any aches and pains? Ask yourself how ambitious this person is. What makes them happy? Do you feel confusion or clarity with their thoughts? What is your clairsentience telling you? What thoughts are being shared with you from spirit helpers? As you feel this shell, feel the texture. Pay attention to all of your thoughts.

Shell Characteristics

Is the shell *smooth*, indicating a smooth pathway at this time? Are you feeling that this person is fully in control of emotions and their life? Do you feel health and happiness around your client? Are they loved and loving? Do you think the pathway ahead will be smooth? Do you feel the client is flamboyant and easy going company? Are you reading for an old soul who is a carer or health worker, someone who gives of their time to help those in need? Let your thoughts wander as you handle this shell.

Does this shell have *spirals*? Is the owner of the shell tumbling through life, having a good time, or are they spiraling out of control? Do they need help to harness their energies? Are they under the influence of someone stronger? Do the spirals indicate growing awareness? Could they be going through a spiritual growth spurt? Could it be that the person is going to mix with more people and have an influence over others' lives? Are they a teacher? Is this inquisitive soul widening their point of view of life on earth and spiritual matters? Are they going round and round in circles, repeating the same lesson over and over? Do they have the ability to go against the odds? Is this person growing continuously through life experiences and working with the energies? Are they able to think on their feet?

Is this shell *fluted like a fan*? Is there a need to learn boundaries? Do they yearn to please others? Are they easily upset? Is this a gentle soul who is happiest when life is balanced and they feel in harmony with everyone around them? Do they go into troughs of happiness followed by patches where they feel alone and miserable? Maybe this shell represents an uncomplicated person who is friendly, popular, and helpful.

Is this *spiky and uneven* shell representative of a prickly person who is hesitant to let anyone get close to them? Have they been hurt in the past and cannot let go of the pain? Are they abrupt with others or untrusting? Can you feel any bitterness or resentment? Can you feel stress? Is greed indicated? Is this person a rough diamond, abrasive on the surface but kind underneath? Are they loud? Does the person cover unease with lots of words, talking non-stop about anything? Are they hypersensitive to criticism and not open to advice? Do they have the need to defend themselves against unexpected hurts? Do they appear to be tougher than they really are? Has this shell been chosen by a uniquely artistic person who is just protective of their skills?

Some shells look like *little caps*. A shell like this would have been brought to you by a homebody who is completely relaxed in their own environment. This would be someone who can keep a confidence. This shell could be the choice of someone who is a dreamer, a person who may not venture far from home and who learns through reading and through the exploits of friends and family. They may be slow to pick up new concepts, but when they do, they follow them through and are totally reliable.

A shell may sometimes look like a *snail*. Does the person who chose this shell hide their true feelings from the world? Have they experienced abuse in the past? Do you feel their lack of confidence? Is this person hesitant to go into a relationship? What advice can you give them to help them move on in life? Do they have a problem mixing with other people? Are they shy and lacking in confidence? Is this person building a home? Do they prefer to be at home with their family? Are they comfortable with going slowly through life, taking small steps but quietly doing well?

Shells Colours

If a person presents you with a white shell, they may be a little naïve, or may be deeply spiritual and have a willingness to embrace life.

A *brown* shell refers to a person who likes to spend time in the garden—someone who is grounded, centered, and reliable.

A *pink* shell tells of lots of love to share. The presenter of this shell is kind and compassionate, continually expressing this to others.

A *grey* shell suggests the owner may suffer with depression or simply prefer their own company. This is a quiet person who likes time alone.

A shell with a *soft, pink underside* would indicate a lovely person who is very loving, trustworthy, and compassionate. This popular person would have empathy and understanding for others. They would love with an open heart, and their home would be a welcoming place to visit. You may feel new love coming for this person or more time spent with the one they love. High principles and good ethics are indicated.

A shell with a *soft, apricot underside* would belong to a very sensual person, one who loves touch, fine fabrics, enchanting music, and art. They would strive to be well-presented and well-spoken. Their home would reflect good taste, and they would enjoy the company of their partner. Sensual people often have shells in their bedrooms to hold massage oils. The shells look wonderful and create a soft and welcoming ambience. The adventurer may like to experiment sexually and be fun in the bedroom.

When a person chooses a shell with a *white underside*, they might be reaching for perfection in relationships, jobs, or spiritual studies, welcoming spiritual advice from spirit, even if they are unsure where it comes from. This advanced soul is very open to learning and to having new experiences. They would be a loyal and honest partner in any type of relationship.

While reading a shell, be very aware of the mind pictures and thoughts that flow through your body. The information may be very subtle, but it is there for you if you concentrate and focus on the shell.

Reading shells can bring some important emotions to the surface. Make sure you have the time to help the person deal with them. It can bring up past life as well as current life issues. It is amazing to see how the gentle energy of a shell can encourage people to talk out their problems in a safe environment.

Sometimes while reading a shell, you will see a future holiday, a reunion with someone this person hasn't seen for many years, or a healing problem that will have to be dealt with in the near future. You may see children or grandchildren, especially if the person is warm and loving and has a caring family.

Ask your guide a lot of questions, and you will soon be in tune with the shell you are reading. Enjoy reading a shell, as it often brings laughter and happy times.

Case Study #1

This reading was for a man in his thirties who had just come out of a marriage. The gentleman chose a small, wide, spiral shell with a white inside. On holding this shell, I could feel this man's pain. He still felt very raw and hard done by. This told me that the parting of ways wasn't his choice and that he was feeling very sad and vulnerable. The spiral represented his good and bad days—days when he could cope and days when he couldn't face the world. I felt that he didn't really have anyone to talk to and that the pain was bottled up inside of him.

As we talked, I could feel his energy lightening up, and he started to look at making plans for a new future. The white inside of the shell showed him that spirit was lighting his pathway and that he could go anywhere and do anything he wanted. We talked about meditating and connecting to his guides for help and advice.

I felt that the spiral would take him to wonderful new places and new people. I saw that in the future he would be motivated and working with positive energy in a new place of work. I also felt that he might do some healing studies, as he had abilities that were mainly untapped. Two changes of career were ahead of him. One would move him to a new area where he would meet new people. A second change would require further training and study and would take him into the world of healing, where he would be very successful and admired for his work.

At some point in time, a wonderful woman would come into his life, one who would bring much happiness and magic.

As always, it would be this young man's choice to make changes or to continue down the same pathway. The reading gave him encouragement, motivation, and suggestions for positive change.

Case Study #2

This reading was for a very slim and attractive eighteen-year-old woman. This young lady vibrated with vitality and good humour. Holding her soft and attractive pink fan shaped shell, I saw her dancing with grace and poise across a stage, and she was compelling to watch. I heard the applause and felt a multitude of feelings from her—great happiness tinged with sadness. She felt vulnerable and elated.

I sensed that her parents were very much against her dancing, and she didn't know if she should proceed to use her God-given talent or obey her parents and work in a shop near the family home.

Dance would bring magic and pleasure, to her and to her future public. The girl was very talented and would go on to making a name for herself in the world of theatre and dance. I felt that she should cherish her freedom and study in the field of her choice to stay on her preferred path. Her life would be filled with wondrous experiences. She had a very good chance of achieving her goals and creating peace in her family. It would be up to her to make her dreams come true, and I felt it had been a privilege to work with her.

Case Study #3

This reading was for a fifty-six-year-old woman, and she chose a snail-shaped shell in muted browns and whites. When this lady passed her shell to me, I felt strong feelings of shame and embarrassment. The browns were dull and uninspired, and I felt that this lady thought she was a failure and had no self-control. She had become cynical and self-doubting over the last few years and was in fact very sad. The snail shell showed that she was lonely and had very little to do with her family, which I thought was caused by excessive drinking. I felt that she had been divorced and that her children saw very little of her. Her life was passing by in a fog, her thinking was very unclear, and bitterness was creeping in.

The white inside of the shell showed the promise of a different future with motivation and self-love.

We talked about the value of Alcoholics Anonymous and where to go to meetings in her area. We talked about freedom and choice, and I encouraged self-appreciation in place of shame. I think she came to me at exactly the right time, as she did join Alcoholics Anonymous and has since been on a world tour with a friend. It is important as a reader to know your limitations and to send people to the appropriate help, counsellors, or groups—if they are ready and willing to remake their lives.

CHAPTER 28

Reading a Lock of Hair

Several people place a lock of hair into an envelope. Each envelope is numbered, and each donor remembers the number they picked. You then draw an envelope to read the hair contained within. Have a notepad handy, and write down your first impressions. Read the vibrations through the envelope first, before you start to read the hair. Choose ten of the questions below, and answer them to the best of your ability. Record what you are feeling or seeing for this person.

Then start to ask yourself questions and record your answers.

What are your first impressions? Do you feel happiness? What do you feel is important in their lives? What are their confidence levels at this stage?

Open the envelope and hold the hair in your hand as you continue to read.

How does the hair feel to you? Is it shiny, brittle, course, soft, or silky? What does this mean to you? Look at the colour of the hair and feel for answers inside of your head about the person who owns this hair. What is your impression of the age of the person you are reading for? What do they do for a living? Is there a change of major importance coming in? Is there something that spirit would like you to share with them? How is the client's health? Are they married or single? What is their occupation? Can you tell them of a very happy event coming up for them? Do you feel the energy of children around them? Do you think they are on a spiritual journey? Where do they live? Do they feel loved? Do they have many friends? What are their interests? Who in spirit would like to connect with this person? Can you give them some messages from their loved ones in spirit?

Who do they need to forgive? What do they need to let go of? Who cherishes them?

What is this person's attitude toward life? Are they strong and reliable? Are they creative? How do they relate to their mother? What makes them proud? Do they like to spend time in nature? Is there an exciting occasion coming up in their life? Do you see any overseas travel for them? Can you name some of the players in their future?

Who spoils them? Who is their role model?

Hair readings are interesting, and they are a challenge. Get a group of people together and see how it goes. You do not need a large lock of hair, so don't scalp your victims!

Case Study #1

I did a reading in a group for a lock of shiny blonde hair. This hair felt beautiful, soft, and well-conditioned. It was vibrant and silky. I felt that the owner was a very happy person, full of the love of life. I felt that this person chased her dreams and made them come true through hard work and persistent effort. I had the impression of boundless energy and optimism, as if this person led a colourful life filled with many friends and happy times. She liked wine and music and fine dining, and she was very good and amusing company. I had a feeling about artistic work—maybe painting or working with fabric. I did not feel that the person had a current partner or that she was in a hurry to find one.

The lady who came forward to claim this lock of hair was in fact a fun-loving silk painter who had us all in stitches with some of her life stories.

Case Study #2

Another private reading of hair that was interesting to do was a lock of salt-and-pepper, black-and-grey hair. This hair was coarse and wiry and had a real no-nonsense feel about it. My first impression was of law and order, of someone who was in the police force or who worked for a security company. There was a definite feeling of "don't mess with me," and I thought it was someone who lived in a black-and-white world with very little compromise. I felt that there was a same-sex partner and that the person had been in this relationship for several years but didn't live with the partner.

Depression and not feeling worthy appeared to be a problem at times. A shield had been built against the world, waiting for the time when she would face criticism from everyone around her. It appeared to me that there were people who knew about her life but didn't interfere in anyway.

The owner confirmed that she was in the police force and that she found it easier to hide her sexual preferences from friends and family. I felt that she was struggling with her life, as it broke a lot of rules in her eyes. She was very sceptical of readings.

A message from her maternal grandmother in spirit cheered her up, as it was sent with a lot of love and acceptance.

CHAPTER 29

Reading Jewellery

Jewellery readings are fairly easy and interesting to do. Open yourself to spirit and allow yourself to feel the energy of the owner of this piece of jewellery. Read with unconditional love and avoid judgment, as you do not know what the client has experienced or the karma he or she is playing out.

Look first at the obvious things. How clean is the piece of jewellery in your hand? This will tell you about the person's self-esteem and the amount of pride they take in their appearance. People who are well-presented will make sure that their clothes are pressed and clean and that their jewellery is sparkling. It is important to them to present a successful and cheerful face to the world, which will reflect their inner being.

If the jewellery is dull and listless, maybe the owner is uncaring about themselves and life in general. They may have low self-esteem and lack control in their own life. Unless the owner is ill and unable to care for their jewellery. They may be stressed and very busy. What suggestion can you make to lift their vibrations and give them the drive and faith to make forward-moving changes?

Is the jewellery old or fairly new? An older piece of jewellery may have had other owners, so you may pick up vibrations from these other people as well as the current wearer. A new piece may still carry the vibrations of the former owner who sold it—or maybe even the jeweller who made it. Let yourself feel for the answers before you start reading for the client.

When you are reading jewellery, use my thoughts as a base and then add your own, as each vibration you read will be different and each answer will be different. I am simply suggesting places to start with your thinking.

Jewellery Characteristics

Broken bits on jewellery may indicate that the piece is not loved. The owner may not be able to afford to fix the piece, or they may have bought a piece that holds no real value to them. It may have been handed down through the family, and if so, it has emotional value. Do you feel the owner lacks self-worth or is despondent or depressed? What guidance can you give at this point that would be helpful?

If the item is a *pendant*, feel the chain, ribbon, or cord attached to it. What does it mean to you?

Gold refers to masculine energy. Maybe the person is heavy with masculine energy or needs masculine energy. Maybe what they need at this time in life is protection from spirit and the gut feelings and strength that are consistent with masculine energy. Gold may refer to success, ambition, higher visions, and the achievement of goals. The wearer may be a very protective person who looks on the bright side of life and has high expectations. Bravery can be indicated, along with a need to provide kindness to family and friends. Gold also resonates with the mental body for practicality and reason. Gold chains show a sunny personality. A gold chain would be good to wear when you need to work with logic and reason.

Silver refers to a person's feminine side. This may be a very feminine person, or perhaps the person needs to strengthen the feminine abilities of nurturing, softness, and intuition. Silver refers to intuition and insight. The wearer may be an elegant and tasteful dresser or decorator.

The owner will have understanding and compassion if encouraged to be the best that he or she can be.

Silver is favoured by readers and highly intuitive people who are seeking answers in the feminine energy. It is a mystical energy, encouraging you to open to your psychic and intuitive skills. It helps you to feel impressions and to reach into the wisdom of the universe. It also teaches us the value of reaching into the silence to balance ourselves and to learn. A silver chain would be good to wear to heighten your intuition.

Remember that we all have masculine and feminine energy and traits. However, some of us are out of balance and may need the opposite energy to bring us back into our spiritual centres.

Ribbons give a necklace a very feminine appearance, indicating softness, openness, and gentleness.

Cords have a more masculine appearance, giving the impression of strength and sending out a silent message: "Don't cross my boundary." Cords may also show the energy of confrontation or control. They are chosen by some because they give the feeling of grounding.

If the jewellery feels *rough*, this may indicate what a person's pathway has been like so far. Maybe it is time to suggest that the person move on in life, letting go of past hurts and forging a new future. It may be time for some self-reflection and restructuring of this person's life. It could also be that the person needs to do some detoxing—drinking more water, eating more fruits and vegetables, and staying away from processed food for a while.

If the jewellery feels *smooth*, the person may set goals and work toward them. This person may be energetic, creative, and hopeful. Life at the present time may be working in their favour due to their own thoughts and efforts. They may have a strong spiritual connection, or may simply be enjoying their journey of discovery on earth.

Does the jewellery *slide slowly through your hands*? If it is slow to move as you try to slide it through your hands, it may indicate a person who is refusing to listen to spirit and who is afraid of change. The client may have many fears to conquer, and you may be able to feel what they are and offer some helpful suggestions. It could be that this person is held back by another person rather than walking their own pathway. Do you feel they are lacking personal freedom? Does their life feel stagnant? Is the energy stuck in old, limiting thought patterns? Can you help them to release some of their worries and offer a new perspective on life? If the jewellery *flows quickly and easily through your hands*, the person is open to positive change and willing to take risks in their life. They like interesting strategies and solutions.

When you hold this piece of jewellery, does it give you *good vibrations* or do you feel a little apprehensive holding the piece? Feel it and allow your thoughts to drift as you tap into the vibration. Your body may react with joy and happiness, or you may experience a sinking feeling in your stomach, giving you a negative answer.

Is the *catch solid, large, and well-formed?* This would indicate that the person is grounded and has a good gateway through which to pass if working with spirit. It could also mean the enquirer is security-conscious and sensible. It may even be a sign of good fortune.

Is the jewellery *rough, tarnished, or small?* Any of these may indicate a problem with personal boundaries, insecurity, vulnerability, and a lack of confidence.

Pendants

Is this piece a *gold icon, cross, or charm pendant?* The gold tells you about masculine energy. Do you feel that the pendant belongs to a male or to someone who needs masculine energy in life at this time? Does this pendant have a religious feel? Are they strongly inclined towards the virtues of honesty, integrity, loyalty, trust, and respect? Do you sense their love for God and humanity? Do you feel unconditional love and kindness emanating from the pendant? Does the gold represent sunshine, laughter, happiness, and a positive attitude toward life? Do you feel that the wearer may need strength, courage, and integrity in an upcoming situation?

Is the jewellery a *silver icon, cross, or charm pendant?* Silver represents the feminine side of our natures. It shows an openness to listen to our intuition, a connection to the divine, and a nurturing attitude to life. It also shows a connection to the moon and the hidden mysteries of life. This may belong to a student of esoteric studies. Silver asks you to eliminate your fears, to release any past life issues holding you back, and to live your life with trust and faith.

Gemstones in Jewellery

Amethyst is a calming stone. It helps to break down stress and to bring in the balance needed in everyday life. It is excellent to wear when meditating or experiencing stress, or when you have a need for tranquillity and inner reflection. It is an excellent healing stone and is a beautiful violet colour. It radiates the same colour violet as the violet healing ray of Saint Germain.

This gemstone would suggest that you talk to them about the stress levels they may be experiencing and offer some advice or suggestions. These could include using lavender or geranium oils, having a regular massage or reiki treatment, learning reiki, reading, walking on the beach, gardening, going to see a funny movie, or having regular holidays. You could mention the effect of amethyst on meditating, as it takes one deeper into the energies and helps you to connect to your inner guidance.

Aquamarine carries feminine energy and is inclined to make you look at yourself. It opens you to a deep understanding of yourself.

You could mention this person's inner child and offer suggestions for clearing old blockages. They may be open to attending empowerment classes or working through old hurts, or they may be ready to delve into a heightened awareness. The lovely, soft blue colour aids relaxation and encourages one to face reality. Is spiritual awareness on a higher level indicated? Are they ready to let go of everything that has been holding them back? Is the wearer ready to look ahead at their destiny and take control of their life? Are they having problems with inner or physical sight?

Bloodstone builds your energy and helps your body to fight infection. It is also excellent for improving your circulation. It is a good stone for grounding and aligning all of your spiritual bodies. It promotes intuition and may dispel confusion.

The wearer of this stone would be a grounded and practical person. They may experience problems with their legs or with cold feet due to sluggish circulation. The owner would develop fairly quickly on a spiritual path, as they would be able to discern personal lessons very well. They would be relatively calm and in control of their life. This kind-hearted person may have an interest in healing or working for the environment.

Blue lace agate is an excellent stone for keeping you calm. It fills your aura with tranquillity and serenity. It is wonderful for people who do public speaking or training of any kind. It brings a smoothness to all communication and encourages patience, tolerance, and tactfulness. It is one of the many stones of protection and may even assist to stop stammering and stuttering.

The wearer of this stone would be trying to improve communication skills at work, in relationships, or in their everyday life. This gemstone promotes kind words and good, clear explanations, and it emanates a soft and gentle energy. Ask about this person's communication skills, and offer any suggestions that may help them. You may also find that they are a little impatient with people who do not think as quickly as they do. This creative person may also be writing a book of fact or fiction or a book for children, or they may be putting together courses. They may attend Toastmasters or take a course to improve their public speaking skills. Think about their communication skills with their family and friends, and let your thoughts form from there.

Carnelian comes in a lot of different hues, from orange to red-brown to orange with tints of red. It is the stone for creativity, fertility, sexuality, and sensuality. In the area of creativity, it replaces negative thoughts with positive ideas and gives you continuous new perspectives. It motivates one to reach for the stars and to have the faith that all will be all right. It moves a person forward in life with a flair for the unusual and opens one to limitless possibilities. Often people who are attracted to carnelian are sensual people who love to be in love and who mix very well with the opposite sex.

You would realize that you were reading for a fun person who takes life by storm and is highly motivated. Let yourself drift into the area of creatively and see what you can find here. You may also be able to find a current relationship or get information on an incoming lover.

Citrine is known as the "merchant's stone," so it brings success, happiness, abundance, and good fortune. It is a crystal that clears negativity from your body and promotes happy thoughts and sound judgement. It promotes psychic awareness and truth in your thoughts and words.

You would read this stone with pleasure, as you would be reading for someone who knows what they want out of life and how to manifest their dreams and expectations. This would indicate leadership abilities and the ability to complete any projects they start. An innovative person who may be interested in business matters, or looking to hear about new opportunities in their working life. You would possibly find that this person has a very balanced relationship with others.

Coral is known for its healing and protective properties. It is suggested for women who want to get pregnant or who are pregnant. It calms the emotions and helps a person to work with intuition. It encourages study and a need for higher wisdom.

Do you feel a pregnancy around the wearer, or the birth of a child for someone who is near and dear to the wearer? Could they be a workaholic, therefore in need of some kind of advice to slow down and take care of themselves. Is the wearer depressed or despondent? Can you give the wearer some new ideas to shake up their life and bring in variety and spontaneity?

Clear fluorite promotes light and clarity in one's life. It helps a person to organize thoughts and to use contemplation and deliberation in the process of creating a future they desire. It helps to balance energies and promotes a spiritual connection.

If the wearer has a pendant with clear fluorite, they are a serious student of esoteric studies. The enquirer has a huge thirst for knowledge and needs to view facts and lessons with clarity. You could be reading for one of the movers and shakers of the world who is extremely intelligent, with a very strong right brain that takes them into the realms of creativity.

Green fluorite aids you when you are emotionally unstable. It helps you to move forward with inner clarity. This gem is associated with heart healing, so it is suitable for someone who is coping with a job loss, broken friendship, or bereavement. You may also tap into their future plans, which will probably include study and a need to move on from a current situation.

Blue fluorite helps you to find practical answers to your questions and helps you to focus through difficult communication. It is excellent for meetings with the boss, for confrontations of any kind, and for keeping you calm when anger threatens to overtake you.

Violet fluorite helps to raise your level of intuition, and it helps with meditation. Violet also helps you to transmute any stale energy you have in your aura or physical body.

Violet connects to your crown chakra, so again we have a student of esoteric knowledge who is seeking the answers to many of life's mysteries. The seeker is looking for a breakthrough in psychic abilities and a stronger connection to the angelic realm and to their spiritual guide. Talk to them about their journey, inner faith, and ability to co-create with the universe.

Yellow fluorite attracts prosperity and abundance. It is like trapped sunlight in clear fluorite, so it makes the wearer conscious of choices and the personal need to reflect their own beliefs. It promotes health, wealth, and happiness, makes a person aware of their own inner rhythms, and helps to build personal power. The person who wears this crystal is on the right path with goals and ambitions and is heading toward prosperity and self-discipline.

Moonstone is often chosen by people who are looking for new beginnings and a fresh start in their lives. It promotes inner strength and inner growth, connects you to the divine, and opens you to a new level of awareness. It builds inspiration and takes you into the void to learn.

The wearer of this lovely gem is ready to take off in a new direction. They would be filled with high expectations and vigour. They have a strong belief in spirit world and may already be a medium or intuitive reader. This mystical person may be looking to travel to raise their consciousness through working with people in different cultures. Moonstone is known to give people safe travel.

Opals promote dream remembrance and help you to manifest your desires. They help you to turn knowledge into wisdom, and they teach you to delve deeply into your inner self. They encourage you to go within for a stronger connection to spirit and to the angelic world.

Again, you would be working with someone who is highly intuitive and interested in rapid growth and self-mastery. Their skills may include clairvoyance, clairaudience or clairsentience. A gentle and nurturing soul would be indicated.

Pearls bring calmness and sincerity into your life. The wearer has faith and integrity in life and presents as a serene and capable person. The person wearing a pearl may be in a position where sound judgement is needed in making future decisions. This person's loyalty may be about to be tested, or they may have the opportunity to increase their feminine energy through courses or fortunate meetings with higher teachers. Channelling is possible for this wearer. They may be involved with charity work, giving their time tirelessly and with grace. They radiate a certain amount of childlike innocence and value their reputation. A cooperative and loyal person who is always prepared to listen.

Rose quartz is often referred to as the "love stone." It promotes sound relationships filled with love, passion, and understanding. It promotes self-love and gives confidence to the wearer. It is very calming, and it releases stress and anxiety. The wearer is a person who loves family and is kind and considerate to children, the elderly, and animals. This is a happy stone, promoting forgiveness and compassion. It balances the emotions and breaks down fear. It also helps one to control a hot temper.

When you read a rose quartz pendant, you may feel the love vibration in your hand, as it has soft, gentle energy and is lovely to hold. The owner may have a new love coming into their life, or might be about to invigorate a current relationship. This lovely gemstone would serve to keep a person calm and balanced, healing their inner wounds and traumas. It would encourage many new friends into the wearer's life, making them popular. Rose quartz is associated with the heart chakra.

Emerald is the stone for transition, taking you into a new and better understanding of life. It will promote deep love and affection. Loyalty will be important to you, and it will possibly attract a new lover who mirrors your journey and will want to work toward enlightenment with you. Wearing this gemstone, you will be much more aware of the plight of humanity, and environmental disasters will rock your soul. You may feel the need to change your job and work with the underprivileged. The rich, vibrant green opens the heart chakra to unconditional love and compassion.

The wearer may be very in-tune with the environment. They may be someone who has a love of dolphins, whales, and other high-vibrating animals. This person is looking for love at a very high level and will not settle for less. Kind and thoughtful, this person would be popular and attract many good friends. Dedicated and sincere, they would be a bonus in the workplace and would always have a need for harmony and balance. They would be good at discerning truth from lies.

The *blue sapphire* improves communication skills and makes a person look deeper into a problem to find the answers. Truth is important, and it will be combined with knowledge, wisdom, and messages from spirit. It takes you into the depths when meditating and is a help with astral travel. It opens your intuition and teaches you to work with faith and trust. The wearer would have the ability to go within to find answers. They would be a sincere and loving person who likes to have their own space and privacy. They would be faithful in a relationship.

The *green sapphire* promotes inspiration and creative thoughts that help the wearer to deliberate answers and to act according to the universal laws. This stone reflects the inner light of the soul and brings many lessons for the wearer. Greater responsibility comes with this gemstone because of the potential for achievement and great spiritual progress. New starts are often indicated—and sometimes a change of residence.

Yellow sapphire improves your memory and takes on-board as much wisdom as you can handle in this lifetime. It helps with concentration and encourages you to study and to find self-expression. It is the gateway to walking a higher spiritual pathway through life. The wearer would be very intelligent and would love to learn and to pass on information. Therefore, this person may be a teacher or work in the field of science. Encourage this person to be free to travel, to learn with great teachers, and then to go out and teach what they have learned. They would normally be a happy person with the gift of wit and laughter to break up heavy moods and confrontations.

The soft, gentle *pink sapphire* promotes love in all of its forms: personal love, universal love, love of children, animals, and the environment, and so forth. It teaches the wearer to stop and listen to what people are saying and to look deep into their hearts for correct answers.

The wearer would be a genuinely good person, someone who cares about family and friends and who would always be available in times of trouble. This person has the ability to step back and let go of control if someone else has the expertise. They are willing to forgive those who have hurt them and, if necessary, to forgive themselves for mistakes they have made in the past. This person is open to the energy flow of love and understanding. They may feel love coming in, or love for their children may predominate their life. They would have high expectations and the inner clarity to make good fortune come their way.

The *ruby* is known for bringing stamina and vitality into your life. It is the gemstone for love and passion, and it helps to remove your doubts and fears. It helps to build your confidence and self-esteem, encourages you to let go of anything that is holding you back, and offers insights and breakthroughs in your thinking. It promotes devotion within. This person would embrace loyalty, joy, opportunity, self-mastery, the forming of solid boundaries, and change.

The wearer may deal with problems from a broad point of view and with laughter and good old-fashioned common sense. This person would be aware of inner rhythms and would be working on improving their patience and grounding. This person would be very responsible and aware that they are co-creating their life. This person would be enthusiastic, setting attainable goals to work toward with energy and courage. Generous and kind-hearted, this person would make an excellent friend and lover. They would be passionate about their partner and about life in general. The wearer may be in a position of power in the workplace, having the determination to succeed against the odds. They would offer assistance to those in need. The ruby is excellent for those who work too hard and push themselves to the limit.

The blue topaz is a stone of protection against psychic and personal attacks from those who are jealous of you. It is an excellent stone to wear when you are doing public speaking or teaching, as it both protects your energy and promotes sound speech. It encourages you to speak with kindness and absolute truth. It recognizes your responsibility as a speaker and the potential you carry to change lives by being a catalyst. It is calming and soothing, and it helps you to manifest through forward movement and inner clarity.

The wearer of this sparkling gemstone would be a good orator. If they are not already working in the field of communications, this would be a sound suggestion for you to make. This person would attract good fortune and abundance.

Yellow topaz is the colour for enhanced wisdom and a strong mental body. It is also for optimism and joy, free thinking, and creative endeavours. It helps to stabilize the emotions and to release long held tension in the solar plexus chakra. It builds confidence and inspiration.

The wearer would be a sociable person who loves to help others and who gives good advice. This person would live life with spontaneity and humour and would probably be very popular. Their laughter may cover a keen intellect and a deep thought process. The yellow topaz breaks down stress and continually works to fill a person with pride and self-empowerment.

Diamonds resonate with the crown chakra and our connection to the divine. They bring harmony and grace into our lives and a strong connection to everyone and everything in our universe. They bring clarity and opportunity, and they amplify our energy and give us vibrancy and determination.

The wearer of a diamond would have sound judgment and an inner balance to help them cope with life. They would be vulnerable and sensitive, open to helping others and enjoy social interaction. They would value trust and loyalty and would be open to working on themselves—cleansing, healing, and rejuvenating. They would be provided with opportunities for prosperity and would experience many discernment lessons. This person may have time in midlife to find their inner person and to build confidence and develop self-expression. They hunger for love and affection and are very loving of themselves.

Rings

Rings come in many shapes and sizes, and they are made from gold, silver, metal, gemstones, and even plastic. Sometimes they are adorned with patterns, nature, or animals.

Dolphins indicate a love of freedom, a need to breathe deeply of life-giving air, and the ability to make decisions in life. They may indicate a love of the sea or simply someone who flows with life's lessons without getting too stressed. Dolphins are said to carry the love vibration on earth, so they are very special creatures. The wearer of a dolphin ring may be a loving and kind person who cares for others and is very warm and protective.

Elephants show strength of character or a need for more strength in decision-making. They are lucky for some and give the inner child confidence. They can indicate someone who is not ready yet to forgive and forget old hurts. They have very long memories and assist students with their studies. Endurance is highlighted, as is stamina. In some cultures, elephants are considered lucky.

Flower designs show a feminine person or someone who needs to bring more feminine energy into life. They show gentleness and deep caring of self and others. The wearers would love music, fine art, and dancing and would be playful and funny. They could be stylish, witty, and popular.

Hummingbirds show that the wearer takes great delight in life, enjoying the little things and having a strong connection to nature and the elemental world. Life is for this person a celebration. They make outstanding friends and they are very loving.

Celtic patterns can represent many things, including aspirations, visions, everlasting love, desire, and anticipation. The wearer is progressive and looking forward to many life adventures, and may be ambitious and eager for new experiences.

Horseshoe rings are often favoured by men, as they indicate a wish for a good life filled with love, happiness, and growth. They are considered by some to be lucky.

Texture and Form of Rings

Rings that feel *rough* may indicate a rough pathway for the wearer, with lots of hurdles for them to cross to get to where they are going. Look into your intuition. You might feel job losses, financial problems, or relationship breakdowns. Possibly the wearer is overcome by the pressure imposed on them by others. It would help if this person focused on solutions and accepted help with appreciation and gratefulness. They may experience emptiness within and be a loner. They may be rough-spoken but have a good heart and compassion for others.

Smooth rings indicate an easier pathway through life, support from family and friends, and lots of happiness. The wheel of life is turning smoothly, and the wearer is confident and cheerful. New opportunities would be viewed with optimism and enthusiasm.

Thick rings show confidence, pride, and a need to be noticed. These people are comfortable in their own skin and enjoy accolades and attention. Stability and determination give them a sense of purpose. They are the achievers who adapt to change and have a vision of what is possible for them.

Thin rings show people who tend to hide themselves behind others, and these people are more often workers than bosses. They may lack confidence or suffer from regular ill health. They hold a lot of their feelings inside, where illness can affect the chakra system. If worn by someone who is boisterous, a thin ring shows someone who is outwardly noisy but lacking in self-esteem. Thin rings may also be worn by someone who has tiny hands. This will then bring in the balance and harmony required in life.

If a person chooses a ring that is *not a circle* but has a flat top or bottom, they are hesitant in life and in making life-changing decisions. The energy flow is blocked, so sometimes they will experience empty patches before the energy picks up and moves again. This person could get very frustrated and bitter if things stop for too long.

The circular shape of a ring stands for eternal life and eternal love, the endless turning of the cycles of our lives, and the love that supports us through our growing and learning stages.

Quick References

A *rough setting around the stones* indicates that the wearer is experiencing difficulty.

One stone could mean a single love and the promise of happiness.

A very *large, single stone* would show a need to be noticed and to be important—unless the wearer has a large hand to balance that design.

Two stones together may indicate a soul-mate relationship—if your feelings are positive. How does it feel to you?

Three stones indicate that the wearer is a good mixer and may enjoy flirting but will not stray from their partner.

For more information on gemstones, refer to the previous section on stones used in jewellery.

Earrings

Earrings are best worn in pairs, as they balance your energy. If, however, you need to wear three or more, you would need the energy to be around your head, brow chakra, and crown chakra. Pretty earrings make the wearers feel special, because they have taken the time to make themselves look good and feel good. Take this into account in your reading. Earrings highlight the face and give radiance to the person.

Bracelets

Solid bracelets indicate that energy is flowing well in the lives of the wearers and that they are on track. Pay attention to the bracelet. Is it made of gold or silver, cloth or rubber. If so, read these elements first. Is the bracelet disjointed, indicating periods of happiness followed by downward patches? Does it have patterns or gemstones? Do you feel that this person is true to themselves and embracing the fullness of their life? Ask your guide for suggestions and ideas to help the person to be perceptive and to have an incredible life filled with love, laughter, and happiness.

Please remember that these are the meanings I work with on a general basis. Always use your intuition, ask your spirit guides for help, and do the very best you can with your reading.

CHAPTER 30

Reading Keys

Reading a set of keys is another way to extend your abilities as a reader. Hold a set of keys in your hand and let the thoughts and feelings flow. Record what you are feeling or seeing as you open further and further for your guides to pass information to you. Ask your guide questions relevant to the owner of the keys so that you can be in that person's energy. Ask if this person is talented, is working in a career that they enjoy, or in a relationship that gives them pleasure? Do you feel some important changes heading their way? Are they in touch with their higher self and on an exciting journey of self discovery? Is this person calm and focused? Are they highly excitable and very talkative?

Key Ring

Is this set of keys on a fancy key ring? Does this make you feel playful and cheerful, or does it make you think of a special holiday? Is it connected to a business logo or a type of car? What does this indicate to you?

Key Characteristics

Square-topped keys lead you to thinking about practicalities, routine, and reliability. This person may possibly have very good self-discipline if they are in the positive aspect of their personality.

They may be honest, truthful, and maybe just a little dogmatic at times. This person can be relied on as a support in tough times and is steadfast in their daily routine. Ask spirit to tell you of an advantageous offer on its way to this person.

If the key you are holding is a *locker key*, what are you feeling? Do your thoughts turn to sport, competitiveness, team or individual efforts, or group bonding? Do you think of exercise, working out, and taking care of oneself? Do you feel anticipation and excitement—or tiredness from this person pushing too hard to succeed? Does this person have special dietary needs? Do they belong to a group or team? Do their fitness levels lead to travel and competition at a higher level? What can you see in their future?

A key with a *pentagon top* would show someone with a very open mind, someone who is responsive to higher guidance. This person may be very balanced and centred, with a good self-image and a loving attitude toward others. They would probably be friendly, fun to be with, and progressive. This person would be a risk-taker and visionary. They would be the leader, if possible, and very much in charge of their own destiny. Give this person the names of three significant people who are coming into their life.

A key with a *rounded triangle top* may indicate that a person has a very quirky personality and views the world very differently from the way others do. This person would be open to travel and learning from other cultures. They would often travel to unusual places in the world and be very non-judgemental of the people they meet. This person may be very spiritual—a seeker of higher knowledge and wisdom—or they may be a thrill-seeker interested in extreme sports.

If the key has a *rounded top*, think about this person's overall journey through life so far. Do you think it has been a fairly easy and good experience? Do you think it will continue in this manner? Do you feel that this person has either strong family ties or strong, supportive friendships? Can you give the age of the owner of the keys, the person's first name, and the name of someone significant?

If you are holding a *car key*, does it feel like this person is in control of their own life? Which states or countries have they visited? Do you enjoy travel or are they happier at home? Name some places where this person spends a lot of time. Have they been on a cruise? Do they enjoy flying? Do you feel that this person's car is well-looked-after? Do you feel that they take time out to pamper and spoil themselves? How high is their self-esteem?

Keys are fun to read. They help you continue your journey—opening to your intuition, connecting to inner guidance, and turning knowledge into wisdom.

CHAPTER 31

Reading a Poem inside of a Closed Envelope

Ask your friend or client to bring a poem in a closed envelope for you to read. If you are in a class, ask that the envelopes be put on a tray, and then let everyone choose an envelope that is not their own.

Hold the envelope between your hands, and remember or write down your impressions.

Your impressions might include love, snow-capped mountains, majestic eagles soaring, brilliantly colourful flowers, the deep blue/green ocean, beautiful long-haired mermaids, powerful animals, dainty fairies, laughing children, new exciting romance, gentle angels, tropical islands, holidays, and so on.

Let the pictures form in your mind, recording exactly what you see. Your first impressions are usually right.

Now work with the emotions. How are you feeling—happy, sad, wistful, eager, full of vitality, loving, caring? Are you experiencing stress and tension? Do you feel very happy holding this envelope?

When you have finished, share your information with the person who put the poem in the envelope. Then read the poem.

Do this exercise regularly, and you will improve as you gain confidence and strengthen your connection to your spirit guide or higher self.

If you want to practice this when you are by yourself, place twelve poems in separate envelopes and put them away for a month. Then read one each day and see how you go. You could also swap your twelve envelopes with a friend's so that you both grow and improve at the same time.

CHAPTER 32

Reading a Drawing of a House

A sk your students or friends to draw a picture of a house. They can take as long as they like and use the colours they prefer.

House Characteristics

A *small house on a large page* indicates that a person feels insignificant, lacks confidence, and has low self-esteem. This person sets limitations on their abilities and may feel unloved or unappreciated. This person may be shy or ashamed of their physical appearance. They may be fighting addictions and may be unable to work with spiritual discipline. This person may be overpowered by someone else and afraid to make their own decisions.

They may be experiencing emotional or physical pain, but feel alone and incapable of reaching out for help. There may be an opportunity to lift this person's confidence and allow them to unload a problem.

If the drawing shows a *large house*, this person would be confident, happy, and balanced. They would have high self-esteem, a purpose in life, ambition, and an expectancy that they will do well. This person would believe in miracles, having an indomitable spirit and the courage to make their life the best it can be. As a leader and one who has the courage to fight for what they want, this person will nearly always get what their heart desires. They can be noisy, happy, fun-filled, and great company. However, they also have the capacity to go into the silence to find answers when in doubt.

If the house in the drawing has *small windows*, the person who drew it may only be seeing a small view of the world. They may not be going out enough to gatherings or having much fun in life. Lacking confidence and feeling inferior and insecure, this person shows a reluctance to be with others except for small amounts of time. They can be overcome by anxiety and fear. Although they may have been brought up to have limited ideas they are trying to live within the boundaries set by their parents. They could also be timid and uncomfortable around others or very private, not wanting others to come too close.

If the house has a *big window*, this person sees the bigger picture and understands that there are many ways to reach goals. They are open-minded and respectful of themselves and others. The artist has an overwhelming desire to achieve and to be successful. This person is filled with positive ideas and is reaching for the stars. They believe they can create magic in their life, and attract prosperity and many rich experiences. This person will be victorious because they believe they can be.

If the house has a *small door*, this person is uncomfortable with powerful people. They are unsure of themselves and need to open their mind to new adventures. It would appear the artist may simply live a modest lifestyle and be happy with that. They may at times feel disconnected and alone. This person is viewing life from the perspective of a mouse and needs to widen their thoughts and ideals. You may be able to suggest areas where this person can make changes that will bring in new and fresh ideas—and new people who will help extend their world.

If the house has a *big door*, this person welcomes friendship. They like to mix with a large variety of people from all walks of life and all cultures. They willingly step out into the world, enjoy travelling, and see every day as a new beginning and a new challenge. This artist copes very well with change, and may change residences many times. Their drawing may indicate that a new opportunity is coming their way, with choices and challenges that will lead to success. Capable and assertive, they will do well in their chosen career. This person believes life is a privilege, and treats everyone with kindness and respect.

A house with *no curtains* indicates an inquisitive person who likes to know what is going on around them. They have nothing to hide and are very open in speech and thoughts. In the positive, they bring light into their life, and in the negative, they may be a stickybeak.

If the house in the drawing is a *mansion*, it shows how this person views themself in relation to the rest of the world. They may feel that they are doing very well and are proud of their accomplishments.

A house may appear *humble* but could also be full of warmth and understanding. Look at the other factors before deciding, and go with your intuition. It may be that this person prefers a humble log cabin to a magnificent mansion, and we are all at our own places on the pathway home to spirit. The feeling coming from this house may be of a person who needs little in the way of material things. In the negative, the person feels that they do not have a lot to offer others, and this is a problem for them. It could also show someone who chooses to live in a poverty syndrome, someone who starts their sentences with "I can't afford"—to buy anything, go anywhere, attend classes, and so on. Sometimes people get stuck in this syndrome and stay there for a long time.

Curtain Colours

Blue curtains indicate a good communicator who may work as a journalist, author, counsellor, care worker, and so on. The artist may shine at public speaking and would make a good mediator. They would also be a good friend. They may suffer with depression if to much time is spent alone.

Green curtains indicate a person who loves the environment and nature, someone who is happy outdoors and is balanced and easy-going. This is someone who enjoys every new challenge life throws in their path and is often fit and healthy. Love is important to this person. They enjoy being in love and are very loving with their partner.

Red curtains indicate a person who likes attention, is bright, happy, and energetic, and has a positive outlook on life. The drawer would focus on family life and spend a lot of time with those who are important to them. They have ambition, drive, and lots of vitality.

Orange curtains identify the house of a creative and sensual person. This person would be a good decorator, having a good feel for decor, colour, music, and food, and would make guests very welcome. This is someone who would have a sensual nature and would be happiest when in a relationship.

Yellow curtains indicate an optimistic person who loves to laugh and play. This is someone who has a very sunny nature and enjoys the company of friends and family. This person's happiness is infectious, and they are very popular. They can keep their boundaries tight and still be honest and loyal in all relationships.

Pink curtains are the colour used by loving and gentle people who love to help others and who have big hearts filled with warmth and compassion. They help many people, and their community speaks highly of them. Champions of the elderly or needy, they are popular and friendly. Their homes reflect the warmth of their natures.

The person who draws *purple* curtains is very spiritual, aiming to make their way through their lessons so they can develop spiritually in this lifetime. They may be a healer or clairvoyant who works to help others. At this person's best, they are dignified and awe-inspiring.

The person who draws pure *white* curtains lives in a state of grace, connected to the divine. This person believes in miracles and divine intervention. They also believe in the power of prayer and self-empowerment. The drawer may be someone who says positive affirmations on a regular basis. Truth would be very important to them.

Outside the House

A flourishing *garden* shows that the person loves life and nature. They use clarity in all situations and look to the future with joy. This garden may belong to someone who sends healing to mother earth or who spends a lot of time in the garden. The person would be someone who is capable of creating peace and comfort in their world.

Trees around the house indicate stability and safety. The artist would be open to growth and new experiences. They would have a love of the earth and might be interested in helping the environment. They may enjoy meditation, breath work, and working with higher energies for advancement in spiritual studies. Also the drawer would be protective and have a wide view of the world.

Red flowers would be drawn by an energetic person who might be ambitious and have strong family ties. The artist is looking to create through dedicated hard work and routine.

Orange flowers indicate a creative person who enjoys romance, special times, and artistic endeavours. This interesting person would enjoy fine dining and fine wine, good company, and special times with like-minded people.

Yellow flowers suggest a joyful person who gets on well with most people and is fun to be with. This person fills their life with optimism and continually looks forward to what is coming next.

Pink flowers indicate a home filled with love, and someone who has much love to share with others. They are often in a relationship or doing many things for family and friends. They are soft-spoken, enjoying quiet times for reflection and study. Expressing a grateful appreciation of life even as they try to understand those around them.

The person with *blue flowers* has a great deal of tact and diplomacy. This might indicate a person who is careful with the words they choose and helpful to others. Talent as a writer or public speaker could be indicated. Their advice would be heartfelt and well worth listening to.

Purple flowers indicate a person with an angelic connection and a strong connection to their spirit guides. They may be clairvoyant, clairaudient, or clairsentient. This is someone who knows that life is a wonderful mystery, and they learn all that they can while on earth. They see all of life as a magnificent gift. They will usually see the beauty in their surroundings and live in gratitude.

White flowers, particularly the rose, show a very strong connection to spirit world. This would show someone who connects to the higherself for answers and strives for perfection.

The presence of *birds* shows progress in life and the ability to find time for oneself and to have freedom of thought. It can also indicate regular visitors or suggest that someone special is about to come into a person's life. Birds may be also be asking a person to look into their problems and challenges from a higher perspective. Birds can bring positive happenings into one's life, transforming learning into success.

Blue sky indicates calmness, happiness, and a positive attitude toward life. A *grey sky* shows a gloomy outlook that can be changed with a positive outlook and positive affirmations. A *thunderous sky* shows incoming arguments and strife. A *rainbow* shows success and happiness.

Put all of these aspects together, use your ideas as well as some of mine, and see what you come up with. If you find that you are feeling a negative vibration, work out what you can suggest to make a person look for happiness and positive changes. Teach the person how to turn obstacles into challenges that can be overcome.

House drawings will give you large amounts of information about people, about how they feel about themselves as they face the world. From this reading, you can make some wonderful observations and suggestions. As you read, explain yourself well so that people understand where your words are coming from. Also, connecting to your guide or their guides will give your reading depth.

CHAPTER 33

Inspirational and Automatic Writing

Inspirational Writing

You will need to sit quietly with a blank page and a pen. Inspirational writing occurs when you meditate and write down the messages from your teacher or guide. You are inspired by their words, thoughts, or pictures to improve your life. It is easy to misinterpret the messages when you begin, but keep trying, and you will become more accurate. Be aware that it would be easy to manipulate the energy and to manipulate others on their journeys. Always work with integrity and honesty.

Messages will not tell you how to run your life, where you need to live, or where you need to work. They will be inspirational, encouraging, and very positive.

You could ask questions like: How may I serve? How can I improve my spiritual understanding? Can you give me ideas on how to manifest my dreams? Can you show me a new perspective on an existing problem? Can you help me to sit in solitude and to still my busy mind? Would you please help me to let go of resentments?

You are fully present in your body and fully conscious during this process. If you are a manipulative person or a controller, this method is not for you, as it gives you the freedom to lie and to make people do what you want them to do. You would also have the opportunity to write bad words about others, blackening their names to make yourself appear spiritual and better than they are. This carries a karmic debt that you do not want to incur.

Clear your mind before you start, and ask your guides to lead you on a pathway of love, truth, and accuracy. This can be a fulfilling experience with lots of new ideas coming your way.

Automatic Writing

Find a quiet place to sit, and ask not to be disturbed. You will need a pen and a blank page to write on. Automatic writing involves giving your arm and hand to spirit to move as they will—to write lessons or give information for your benefit or for the benefit of others. You place your essence slightly off-centre to allow the presence of a spirit person to write through you. Keep your arm light, and do not rest it on anything.

To begin, hold your pen lightly on a blank page. Allow the pen to move in circles as it is directed by spirit. Gradually, words will start to form.

Please note that messages from spirit are positive and uplifting. There will not be any swearing or negativity or any attempt to run or rule your life. If your message is from the light, you will only experience support and new information to promote your personal growth.

You could ask questions like: How do I recognize my spiritual gifts? Can you suggest how I can improve my sense of humour and see everything in my life as a lesson? How can I improve my confidence? How will breathing exercises help my development? How do I forgive someone who has hurt me very badly? Am I on my wisest path? How can I improve my focus in the future? How can I overcome my cravings for sweet foods, cigarettes, alcohol, or drugs? How can I attract prosperity? How can I attract a new love into my life? Can you help me to be more spontaneous? What are my totem animals?

You may feel like you have entered a slightly different state of consciousness while doing automatic writing. When you have finished, thank your guide for the help, and sit quietly while you absorb the information.

CHAPTER 34

Reading Faces

Face Shapes

Face-reading starts with the shape of the face. Look to see if the person has a long, square, oval, or round face. Read the following points to help you to read faces.

A *long* face would have prominent cheek bones, giving an aristocratic appearance at times. This person may have hollow cheeks and attractive eyes. Usually you would notice a strong, well-defined nose, giving them the appearance of being strong and capable. This person meets your eyes when you speak to them and has good listening skills with good comprehension. They are usually a good judge of character and are often found running their own business or in a management position. Possessing good self-discipline, this person is known for being a good leader and planner with strong and creative ideas. They work hard to achieve their dreams, and friendship is valued. A strong jawline shows determination, confidence, and a willingness to try new experiences. In the negative, this person may be bossy or controlling.

People with *square* faces are usually very reliable and stable, possessing analytical minds and strong opinions. They can be resistant to making big changes, and they like to buy their own homes and settle in. They are fair with their co-workers, partners, and children, although they can be a little strict at times. They put a lot of pressure on themselves to perform and will work hard until each job is finished, making them valued employees. They are good at saving money. They tend to return to the same place for holidays, as they like to understand and know their environment. They strongly believe in justice and a fair deal for everyone, and they will stand by friends in need. In the negative, they may dominate others, and they always like to have their own way.

An *oval* face indicates a good sense of humour, and people with oval faces like to work hard and play hard. They have lots of friends, and they love to party and socialize. They are gracious hosts, and it is a pleasure to be invited to their homes. They are attentive as partners and are usually faithful in relationships once they fall in love. Their lives are filled with joy and eager anticipation for the next adventure, as they are very appreciative, full of fun, and at times restless. They may be very creative and talented in the artistic fields, and many are on a journey into self-awareness and self-empowerment. These people have an abundance of energy and love to share. In the negative, they can rush into relationships with disastrous results, and they are hypersensitive to criticism.

People with *round* faces have soft eyes filled with humour. They are kind and caring and very sensitive toward others. They have great tact and diplomacy, can solve most problems, and are gentle in their attitudes toward others. Good communication skills make them valued in groups or as counsellors and diplomats. They tend to overwork, and they may be seen as reliable and safe parent figures in groups. Sociable and friendly, they can be overly emotional, taking on the problems of others. These people are often psychic and have many skills in the healing field. In the negative, they possess weak personal boundaries. They work endlessly on behalf of others, and demanding people drain their energy and leave them feeling flat.

Facial Characteristics

Chins

A *pointed* and strong chin indicates a person who is independent, ambitious, and energetic. A master of their own destiny.

A *weak* chin indicates weakness in health and in holding one's ground during disputes and arguments. Someone with a weak chin would be happy to follow others, and likely to lack ambition and drive.

A *protruding* chin shows determination and the ability to travel or work on one's own. This person would be the dominant partner in a relationship, but would also be very caring and nurturing.

Lips

Full lips show passion, laughter, strong sexuality, affluence, and financial gains.

A *thin top lip* indicates possible ill health—or that money problems will play a big part in this person's life.

Thin lips indicate a person who likes to think deeply and solve problems. These people are analytical and thorough in everything they do. They can be relied on in difficult times.

Eyebrows

Thick, *strong*, and *large* eyebrows indicate a dominant personality with the strength to follow one's dreams. This person may be controlling or aggressive at times. This feature indicates the "warrior" energy.

Fine eyebrows show a person who is proud of their appearance and sensitive toward others. This person's mind is always active, and they are a good judge of character. They would have refined taste and like to be with like-minded people.

Straight eyebrows belong to no-nonsense people who are always on-the-go. They like to be kept busy, are at times abrupt in their speech, and can show impatience.

Pointed eyebrows are straight and then dip downward. These indicate intuition and high levels of sensitivity. They show that a person is innovative and creative and are often found in spiritual people who work in this field.

Bushy eyebrows can indicate a person who has a problem with being tactful. They may be a little too opinionated and forceful.

One, *long continuous* eyebrow shows someone who is a worrier, someone who is always trying to please others and get it right. There might be a problem with stress or depression. They need to take regular breaks from work, and holidays are important to their general health.

Foreheads

Lines between the eyebrows show worry, stress, and strain.

Wide foreheads indicate practical, hard workers with good common sense. They give good advice and are sought after as friends.

Narrow foreheads tend to indicate family or relationship problems. The person may find or create many obstacles in life, and may have lots of lessons to learn.

Ears

Close-set ears show a cautious person who isn't interested in taking big risks. They would like home life and plan activities well ahead. This would indicate a more conservative type of person who saves well and likes comfortable surroundings.

Large ears indicate a very independent personality with strength and innovative ideas. This type of personality is better suited to a boss role than an employee role, and is usually mentally very active.

Small ears belong to sensitive people who work with gut feelings and intuition. They are great observers of life and of people, and they are usually good judges of character.

Eyes

Happy, *sparkling* eyes show that the person loves to joke and have fun. They might be a flirt and mix well with both sexes.

This is someone who loves to be with others and is very sociable. They would live a happy, carefree life and not take themselves too seriously.

Eyes that are *close together* may indicate a narrow vision of life and ideas that are set from a young age. Such a person may have tunnel vision and be very determined to do things their own way.

Eyes that are *far apart* belong to broad-minded people who are always open to new challenges. They thrive on challenge and change, and they are interesting to be with.

Deep-set eyes look mysterious and belong to people who are deep thinkers with romantic hearts. They are good judges of character and may be a little serious. They have the ability to be successful and prosperous. Deep-set eyes can also indicate ill health.

Face reading is fun to do, and as you work, you will get a lot of intuitive thoughts to pass on.

It is interesting to see who will look you in the eye with honesty and interest, and who will look away, unsure of what you will find. Be kind, work with humility and grace, and make the experience empowering for your client.

Sample Reading

I did this reading for a lady with a round face, sparkling eyes, a strong jawline, high-arched eyebrows, and ears close to her head.

This lady's appearance would indicate to you that she is a happy and light-hearted person who is a good friend and an equal partner in a relationship. She is joyful and easy to be with. She has a streak of determination and is able to hold her personal boundaries. She is able to cope with the unexpected and makes light of her good deeds. She is intuitive and sensitive to the needs of others, true to herself, and living in faith.

CHAPTER 35

Reading a Drawing

This is a lot of fun. Ask your client to work with pencils, markers, crayons, white or coloured paper, sparkles, or stickers to draw a picture. They may add words or anything they want to make it an interesting project. Using their imaginations, they create their own masterpieces for you to read.

Refer back to the chapter on reading a house, and then consider the additional information.

People

Look at the *size* of the people in this drawing to find their importance in the artist's life. Pay attention to how they are dressed and the colours of their clothes. How many people are prominent in this picture? Has anyone been placed in the background? Are there any children? Are there any pets? What interests do you think the artist has? What do you think is the most important thing in the life of the artist? Do you think this person has strong boundaries? Would this person be fun to be with? Are they happy? Do they feel lonely?

Which part of the picture represents negativity?

On which colour has the artist placed the sparkles? Where would this person like to shine? Which stickers did they choose, and why do you think they were important? Is it a soft picture or a vibrant picture? Can you find something positive in this person's future? What is the proportion of the picture to the size of the paper? Discuss your thoughts and feelings with the artist to help them on their life's path.

Sample Reading

The picture you are given to read has purple mountains in the background, a gentle stream rolling through the middle of the picture, girls playing with a maypole on the left-hand side, and people having a picnic on the right. The sky is predominantly blue with some small grey clouds drifting into sight. The sun is shining and creating shadows by a large lush tree. There is a man who is happy and smiling, a seated lady who is making a daisy chain, and another young man watching them. There's a small brown dog with the people, and there is a black rabbit looking on.

The lovely blue sky would suggest calmness and everyone at peace on this lovely day. The small grey clouds may indicate some problems coming in at a later date, but they are not a big problem now. The mountains represent spiritual advancement and integrity, and they offer hope for the future.

The tree, lush and beautiful, creates harmony and balance for all who share its shade, and it refers to the growth of the people in this picture. It is encouraging them to manifest their hearts' desires with integrity and honour. If it has green leaves, it is offering new opportunities for study or new adventures that involve the heart. It encourages balanced relationships built on love and respect, which represent one's highest good and choices made with spiritual wisdom.

The children at the maypole represent happiness, spontaneity, and joy. The children are laughing and getting on well together, enjoying this pleasant outing. There is a general feeling of happiness. However the grey clouds ahead may give warning of unexpected change.

The woman is comfortable and demure, as she knows she has the interest of two different men. One of the men shows confidence, while the other is more hesitant but nonetheless interested. The eternal triangle is being played out. The lady may have a moral choice to make in the near future. The dog indicates loyalty and may be a hint for the lady. The rabbit suggests an opportunity to let go of morals and to take a chance elsewhere. However, the colour of the rabbit may indicate the outcome of this action.

Use your clairsentience to feel how you think this drama will be played out. Offer helpfulness and encouragement. It would appear to me that the outcome is up to the choices made by the woman, which need to be made with honour and in a state of grace.

CHAPTER 36

Reading a Watch

old the watch in your hand and sit quietly for a few minutes. Remember or record the information you are given. Now, play with the watchband and see what information comes to you from it. Does the band feel smooth or rough? What does this indicate to you?

Read through the following descriptions and get a feel for which comments are right for the watch you are holding.

The Watch

The owner of a *gold* watch is someone who is relatively strong and capable. They have the capacity to listen, learn, and then act. They would be known to have tenacity and endurance, courage and stamina. They may be someone who can discriminate and who has the courage to go out there and make life happen. The gold watch shows purpose and ambition, the owner will possibly mix well socially and be fairly popular. They are capable of setting goals and reaching them.

If the watch is scratched and shabby, the owner has lost some of their self-empowerment, and you may be able to help them lift their spirits and get back on track. If the watch no longer works, find out when time "stood still" for this person. They may be stuck in a negative situation.

A *silver* watch may belong to someone who doesn't necessarily stand out in a crowd. They may have a quieter personality and tend to sit back to listen and learn from others. They could be intuitive and nurturing toward others. They may have an interest in spiritual learning or books, go to spiritual classes, or teach classes. This person knows how to create peace in their life, and can adapt to change without drama. They are a natural problem-solver.

Pause every now and then, and let your spirit guide give you information. Then, when there is silence, go back to the feel of the watch to keep yourself in the energy and working.

The Watchband

Leather is usually the choice of very sensible and reliable people. They have trust, and they work with faith and indomitable spirits. They are very grounded and centred and try to stay in balance through all of their challenges.

Does the watchband have a *firm, strong clasp*? Perhaps this would mean to you that the person is safety-conscious, values their things, or likes this particular piece of jewellery. A *weak clasp* shows indecisiveness.

The Face

A *round* watch face indicates a softness in the owner, a willingness to help others and to spend time with children, the elderly, and with nature. The wearer would love to laugh and be sociable, and they are often very popular with others. They would be respectful of others, and might be a visionary full of potential and faith. This person would be very flexible with their own ideas and also open to new ideas.

A *square* watch face would be chosen by someone who is punctual, efficient, and practical. The owner is confident and lives life with a purpose. They have mental clarity and an aptitude for many things. They are able to break through the lies and discern the truth of a matter.

An *oblong* watch face is often chosen by a high achiever who sets goals and reaches them. This is worn by someone who would make an excellent boss, and is dedicated to their family and job.

Fancy watch faces are chosen by people who are artistic and who love texture, pattern, and design. These people have a love of colour, fabric, music, and fine wines or fine foods. They may enjoy the theatre or be in the theatre, and they could be artistic or musical.

A *plain* watch face indicates a certain need to go back to the basics in life. Someone with this style of watch would probably speak their truth and would not like to be kept waiting. They value honesty and integrity and make sound friendships that often last for a lifetime.

Scratches on the face may indicate that the wearer is very tired or stressed. The owner simply may not have enough time to keep up with current responsibilities and is in need of a holiday or simply time out.

Time

Look at the time on the watch face and see if the numbers mean anything to you—perhaps an appointment time, an age, or a birthday. You may feel that it is time for the person to make changes that would be beneficial to them or to their family or business.

Feelings

How do you feel when you hold this watch? Is there a feeling of calm or of worry? Does this person seem to be coping with life, or are they unhappy and depressed.

How does this person act when faced with adversity? Is the person brave in the face of danger? Do they create dramas to play out, or do they have a sense of honesty and dignity? Is this a person who likes flattery? Do they feel grounded? What is this person's major weakness? Can you offer suggestions for change?

Use my ideas to start the thought process, and then leave it to spirit to give you any details they think are important for that person on that day. It is important to hand over the information exactly as it is given to you. Although it may mean nothing to you, it may mean a lot to others.

CHAPTER 37

Reading a Drawing of a Tree

Ask your class or friend to draw a picture of a tree in five minutes. Leave the colour choices up to them. When they have finished read the picture.

Tree Characteristics

First look at the *size* of the tree on the page. This tree represents the person's life journey so far, and the size of the tree tells you about their self-confidence and level of self-esteem.

Trunk

The *size of the trunk* is also relevant. Look to see if it is solid and grounded. A *tall* tree could mean that the person is reaching for awareness. They may be very active, ambitious, or eager to learn. They have a wider view of the world and are fairly open-minded. The artistic person loves and respects themselves and others. If the tree is *short*, it represents slower progress, a lack of ambition, or an intentionally quiet life without the need for progress. Living with self-imposed boundaries they would have a need for proof of everything. There would also be a strong need for security and safety.

If the tree is *gnarled* or *knotted*, it refers to difficult times and challenges for the person to overcome. Life will not be a smooth journey. The artist may be working off some karma or may encounter serious illness or accidents along the way. They may be a little stubborn and refuse to let go of past slights.

A *slim* tree indicates flexibility and someone who can shift their consciousness when necessary, therefore they do not always need to be right and are open to many ideas. They are a quick thinker and enjoy learning about new places and people.

A *huge* tree indicates a person who has lots of stored information but hasn't done a lot with it yet. The drawer might be bursting with things they would like to do, but hasn't had the opportunity to do them yet. They may also hold on to wounds, not yet ready to deal with them. A huge tree may indicate someone with a need for security, routine, and discipline as part of their daily life.

Branches

A tree with *many* branches indicates many choices for the drawer to make. Many pathways are open to this person for learning their lessons. There will probably be good support along the way. The artist might give shelter to others who are weaker and in need of support.

A tree with *few* branches indicates a relatively limited life, but if the branches are strong, there is a good chance the artist will do well. If the branches are weak, they may have problems with indecision, a lack of nerve to carry through on ideas, or depression.

A person who draws *twigs* likes fine detail and reads the fine print. This could also indicate health problems or a tendency to let little things annoy them. They could also be fickle with affections, lacking steadfastness. They may be good at starting projects, but may not finish them. Twigs could indicate that the person is impatient and does not suffer fools gladly. On the flip side, this person is fun-loving and has little concern for tomorrow. They are a joy to be with and quite popular. Go with the feelings you have on twigs.

Leaves

Light-green leaves indicate someone who welcomes new starts. They are filled with enthusiasm, and love challenges, new people, and new places to go. It would represent someone who is on a journey of enlightenment. They present as bright, friendly, and happy. A popular person who mixes well with others.

Dark-green leaves indicate that a person is more settled in their life. They have security and a good connection to their family, and they strive for balance and wisdom. Looking deeply into their life they may find as time goes by they are interested in raising lots of children. They may work with special needs children or help to look after the elderly.

Gold leaves show a good connection to the divine energy, inner clarity, and the releasing of the old to make way for new energy and happenings. People who draw gold leaves are looking for gateways of opportunity, and they will often be very successful, helping a lot of people and amassing a lot of money along the way. Travel may be indicated here as a preferred way of learning. Filled with curiosity they would enjoy other cultures and learn from everyone they meet. Interested in study, they are strong, self-assured, and capable.

Red and *russet* leaves indicate leadership abilities, good self-expression, and a strong life force. These people are able to break through their barriers and make an active difference in their lives and the lives around them. They would probably be vivacious and appear larger-than-life.

A plush tree with *lots of leaves* indicates a very busy life. The person who draws this tree fills up every minute of their life and is only happy when doing something and staying busy. It could also indicate someone who has an innate need for privacy (as one who hides behind the leaves).

A tree with *few leaves* could point to a lack of confidence. Not many things happen in this person's life, and they lack the stamina to make life happen in a bigger way. This drawing can indicate a person who has few interests or who is lazy.

A tree with *no leaves* represents the barren and lonely life of someone who doesn't mix well and who spends a lot of time at home. The possibility of a lonely heart is indicated—one that would welcome a partner or good friends. There is a feeling of uncertainty about this person's future plans.

Root System

A *strong* root system indicates a person who is very grounded and stable. Someone who would deliberate before committing to a new project. They are likely to offer assistance to others and build solidly on their dreams. They would be strongly connected to the rhythms of life and to mother earth. They are responsible and caring, encouraging others to find freedom through inner growth. They may attract the weak and needy and may form co-dependent relationships.

A *weak and spindly* root system indicates a person who may lack confidence and may be a follower rather than a leader. They may have a strong friend or partner. The artist may be kind and caring, but may not have the tools at this stage to be effective and productive in their life. Lack of grounding is indicated, along with a need to open their world and find true potential.

Background

The person who adds *blue sky* to their drawing is filled with sunshine and laughter and has very high expectations. They look for new adventures and challenges. As a good communicator, this person would be an excellent teacher, mentor, or lecturer.

A person who uses the colour *grey* in their drawing may suffer from a lack of self-esteem and possibly depression, being unable to look on the bright side of life. Instead of making positive changes they tend to be a pessimist and complain frequently. They are someone who makes you feel miserable after a short time in their company. They expect you to pick them up when they are down, and they don't even consider that they are draining your energy. The darker the grey in the picture, the bigger the problem. This is probably only short-term, and you may be able to offer assistance.

A picture that contains the *sun* is drawn by an optimist, one who welcomes each day with eagerness and excitement. This enlightened person is able to make a bad situation into a good one and is willing to share their love and laughter with others. They could be fashionable, excellent with colour and style, and enjoy celebrations and being with others, but can also be equally happy with their own company. Possessing an inexhaustible supply of energy, they are fit, healthy, and vibrant. Achievement and successful completion of study are indicated in their life, as they are an active person with a thirst for life and knowledge.

Mountains in a drawing indicate a person who is looking to improve life and grow spiritually. Aiming for the peaks they are prepared to walk a long, slow journey, as every step of the journey is a revelation to them. They aim high and usually achieve everything they set out to do or be. Snow on the mountains shows higher spirituality.

A *river* in the drawing shows that strong emotions may rule this person's life. They think with their heart and are easily hurt, you will find they are also compassionate towards others who may be suffering. This may indicate someone who has a need to be all-knowing in the lives of others and could appear to be bossy or overbearing. They might cry easily or have temper tantrums, or might be very volatile and possibly restless. They may possibly have a problem letting go of old lovers or people who have hurt them, even if the hurt is imaginary. They hold grudges and can be morose. They may carry a lot of fluid and their body is filled with stagnation or bitterness and resentment.

A *stream* in the drawing indicates a person with balanced emotions and a kind nature. With a lively and cheerful personality, they would be inspirational and personable. They can keep their emotions in check. Living with a life filled with merriment, empowerment, enjoyment and happiness, they would be fun to know.

A *dry river bed* shows a person who is depleted at this time in their life. Can you offer some positive words to encourage this person to make changes?

Birds in the sky indicate a person who is looking to see the overall picture, one who will always be a student of life, willing and eager to learn and protective of those they love. Working with inner guidance they would also be connected with the angelic world.

When the artist has finished the drawing of the tree, you could ask them to rule a horizontal line through the tree. This would give you an idea of how far along the journey they are depending on the position of the line and how far it is up the tree. This person may have had many lives, or may still have many more lives yet to come.

Sample Reading #1

This drawing was done by a twenty-five-year-old student who was studying to be a chiropractor.

The picture has a tree that is tall and slim, with a strong root system and light-green leaves. The background is a light-blue sky with a sun and two birds flying high. There are mountains in the background with purple and white peaks. Over all, the picture looks happy and light with energy.

This young man has his world before him and is anticipating success. He is a capable student who is following his dream. The purple and white in the mountains show that this person is spiritual and aiming for the best results he can get. The two birds indicate that he has a partner or is looking for a partner to share his journey with him. He enjoys learning new things and is open and flexible with his study. There is a strong feeling of success—that he is capable of manifesting the life he desires. The sun would indicate successful completion of study.

Sample Reading #2

This picture was drawn by a fifty-five-year-old woman, six months after her marriage separation.

It is a short, stunted tree in a bare paddock with no colour in the sky. The leaves are a sage-green, and there aren't many of them. The root system has been overlooked. The overall feeling is of sadness and loneliness.

The lack of self-esteem is the first thing I would see here. The lady feels like her life was cut short and is, in fact, over. She is suffering with a nervous disposition (the sage-coloured leaves) and is not ready to go out alone and face the world. Look into your inner self and see what might be coming up for this lady—new friends, new places to go, or a new partner further along the way. You may see her attending engagements or weddings, holding a new baby, or just being out to dinner and having some fun.

It would be important to talk to this lady about how she can make changes in her life. Give her ideas of things to do and ways to find inner peace—through meditation, spiritual churches, good friends, or laughter during a movie—to lift her spirit. Suggest that she work with positive affirmations to change each negative thought into two positive ones. It would also help her to put a list of things she is grateful for on her refrigerator where she can read it every day—starting with things like being grateful for good health. You could suggest that she visit a spiritual counsellor. Maybe she could learn reiki and join a group of people who meet regularly to work on each other. Encourage her to mix more and to help other people—maybe through working with charities which could include helping the elderly or something similar, where she would have a commitment and somewhere to go each week.

Meditation

A small meditation may help to connect this person to the things you are seeing. Guide her through the following exercise.

Close your eyes and relax. Imagine that you have melded with the tree in your picture. Enjoy the stillness and feel the heartbeat of the tree. The heartbeat connects the tree to mother earth and to her rhythms. Feel as if you are at one with the universe.

Let your energy flow down into the roots, the place of your past lives and the things you need to let go of. What can you release at this time? Who can you forgive so that you can move forward in your life?

Can you feel the child that you were in this lifetime? Can you give that child a hug or warm wishes and make them feel special?

Take your consciousness up higher into the tree. Can you feel the sun shining on you, giving you life-giving warmth and care? Can you tell the sun how grateful you are for the support that is coming your way?

A bird lands gently on one of your branches. What kind of bird is it? What do you want to say to the bird, who is a representation of someone in your life? Are you happy to have them there? It would appear that they have something they wish to say to you. Take a minute to listen to what they have to say. Pause.

A little animal scurries around at the base of the tree. It has a message for you. What is it?

Now, take your energy to the very top of your tree. Feel the wind swaying you, and feel the connection you have to everything and everyone on this planet. Let your consciousness reach out to the universe, and imagine the home you came from in another dimension. Let some pictures form in your mind.

An eagle flies overhead to let you know that it is a good thing to look from above and see the bigger picture and to make your own decisions. You are a free child of the universe, much loved and capable of doing your earth lessons.

Stay for a couple of minutes in your tree and feel the heartbeat working in unison with yours. Feel your body relax, and know that you have the strength of the tree, a connection to the divine, and that you are loved. Share your talents with others, and reconnect to the world in a bigger way.

CHAPTER 38

Reading Auras

Seeing the Outline

When you are reading someone's aura, it is helpful to have them sit or stand in front of a white or cream-coloured wall to enhance the auric colours. We all have a blue or white outline around our bodies, and this is what you will see when you start to do this exercise. Ask your guides to help you.

Stand quietly and stare into the person's third eye for several seconds. Then raise your gaze to just above the person's head, turning your head slightly to the side, and squint. You will see a white light forming around the body. Repeat the exercise several times, and you may see colour start to form around the head. Change your focus and stare into one shoulder for several seconds. Then raise your vision just above the shoulder, turning your head to the side and squinting.

You will see the white light form around the shoulder. With practice, you will see the colours start to form. This exercise requires a lot of practice, but it can be done by most people in time. As you turn your head to the side, you are seeing with many more of your eyes' colour-sensing rods than when you are looking directly at the person. Squinting softens your vision and helps you to see the colours.

Aura Colours

If the person you are reading for is healthy, you will be viewing strong, bright colours that look like they are illuminated by light—much like the colours of a stained-glass window with the light behind it.

The colours mean different things to different people, but I will share with you the meanings my guides have given me.

An abundance of *bright red* in an auric field suggests that there is a lot of energy. We would be looking at a person who has enthusiasm for life, ambition, drive, and may enjoy sports for an adrenaline rush. They love excitement and enjoy the company of people with similar thoughts and hobbies. Well dressed and intelligent, they attract the eye of the opposite sex. You will find they enjoy family ties and often have good-looking partners.

A darker, *muddy red* colour in the aura may suggest a problem with high blood pressure and light-headedness. Arguments may be common for this person, and they may have a problem with their temper and impatience with people who think slowly. Road rage and insensitivity toward others could also be shown here. Sometimes this colour shows a controlling energy and an abusive person.

Clear orange in the aura shows a very creative and imaginative energy. An artistic person who has the ability to work with decorating, style, or art is indicated. They are very open to ideas and suggestions from spirit. They are usually fertile and sensual and have a good sense of self. Possessing good taste, they may have the energy of the author, artist, sculptor, or dancer. Cooking may be one of their skills.

A *muddy orange* aura indicates a person with heavy energy, someone who speaks roughly and possibly enjoys pornography. They may be manipulative and could be a bully. This lonely individual is yet to find true love, and usually their love is based on a need to control others. They could have a problem with jealousy or envy, be overly sexual, or lack any sex drive at all.

A *bright, clear yellow* aura indicates a person with a sunny personality whose optimism makes them popular. They would make an interesting public speaker, a fun-filled friend, and wonderful partner. At peace with themselves, this person is confident, honest, and mentally alert. They have an analytical mind and learn from everyone who crosses their path. A joyous and happy person who sees life as a wonderful gift.

Muddy yellow indicates problems with confidence and self-esteem. Dishonesty could be indicated both with themselves and with others. Stress may also be shown, as the person may live in the victim archetype.

Lots of new, creative, and imaginative ideas come in with *clear green* in the aura. This would indicate a kind and compassionate person who believes in miracles and feels with their heart and soul. They are known for their empathy and understanding and are very caring and loving of those in need. The clear green aura shows an older soul who recognizes synchronicity, cooperates with others, and may have a healing touch. Appreciative of life and willing to share their time and gifs with others, we would be looking at a popular and well-loved person. They may help others financially in this lifetime, with no thought of repayment and no strings attached.

Muddy green is the aura colour of an insensitive and disenchanted life. Such a person may be stuck in the past because of a broken heart over a recent relationship. They are not ready for or open to new love, as they may be stuck in the "poor-me" syndrome, causing them to be selfish, jealous, or gossipy.

Clear blue is found in the aura of a person who is happy to communicate with others. Their skills would include speaking with clarity and listening intentively. Open to spontaneous change, they may be thinking about changing their job or buying a new home. There would be good decisions made after sound research. This indicates someone who enjoys good health, challenges, and truth in all areas of life.

People with *muddy blue* in their auras talk over the top of others. They are not good listeners, and they have a great sense of self-importance. They have a need to always be right and can be nitpickers who take the joy from others. Dogmatic and often vain, they are intellectual snobs.

Clear indigo indicates the talents of clairvoyance, clairaudience, clairsentience, and knowing. There may be a great deal of light behind the indigo, as this person's aura is filled with spiritual light, indicating a high level of integrity, high morals, and a good reputation. This self-empowered person would be brave enough to make controversial choices. They are very accepting of their inner transformation, and since they can appreciate that altering their own thoughts changes their destiny, they are already on their spiritual journey to enlightenment.

Muddy indigo indicates the false "guru" who is looking to have devotees. The false "guru" is on the journey of the negative ego and needs praise and adoring followers. They would lack integrity and may be a false prophet.

A very spiritual person would have *violet or white* in their aura, and they would be at peace with themselves and the world. Believing in the power of prayer, this enlightened person also believes in miracles and has high expectations of themselves and would-be healers and teachers on this planet. They are able to find the deep space within their heart to help heal the world, master their thoughts, and be at one with the universe. This person has transformed into a better person through dedication and hard work. They have a strong connection to spirit guides and angels.

A *white orb* is the presence of a spirit guide or a spirit person. It can often be seen in photos or over the shoulder of the person you are reading for. These orbs are often referred to as "spirit light." They are often seen around working mediums.

An incoming illness or a past life that needs to be cleared shows up in the aura as a *black patch*. It may also be caused by bereavement and sadness. It could occur in the aura of someone who is very depressed or out-of-balance.

Exercise

Ask your guide or angel for help as you draw a friend's aura. Feel the colours if you cannot see them. Keep your reading friendly and uplifting, and encourage the person to make good choices that will lead to a happy life.

CHAPTER 39

Mediumship

Mediumship involves working directly with spirit, linking to people who have passed from this life and who want to send messages to the loved ones they have left behind. This is a very sensitive area to work in, as you will be dealing with people in pain who may have high levels of stress. Be very sure that you have the correct connection and information, as these people are relying on your truth and integrity.

Mediumship was part of my life when I was younger. Life choices and illness made me step back from this journey, and I only did a bit of this work until recent years. Now, working again in this field brings me much pleasure, and I hope to comfort those I read for.

Breath work is a way of calming the mind and going into the open spaces where spirit can communicate. You will need to lift your vibrations, as spirit people lower theirs to meet you in the middle.

Mediums usually work with people who are grieving and experiencing great emotional pain. Clients come to you, usually within a year of losing a loved one. It is advisable for them to wait at least six months for their energy to settle and the healing process to start. The grief is so hard for them to bear, and it is the responsibility of the medium to be accurate and compassionate. Often the spirit person connects to you before their relative arrives, sometimes bringing with them a family pet that has passed over. I think this is a way to further validate that you are speaking to the correct person. Sometimes the person you are looking to connect with doesn't come in, or comes in later, so someone else will be the first contact you have with spirit world for your client.

As my grandparents, father, brother, and favourite aunt have passed into spirit, I have walked the walk of the bereaved, and I know from experience how gut-wrenching it is. While we have a belief in spirit world, we miss the physical presence of those we love when they pass to the other side.

Confirmation from a good medium is such wonderful solace. My parents had to cope with losing their twenty-two-year-old son, and my heart breaks for other parents who have this experience.

We all have to leave this planet, but in this society, it is something that we choose not to think about. Bereavement is a very hard lesson, and it takes a long time to accept it and to realize that the soul continues its journey in a different place. If we have the understanding that we will meet our loved ones again on the other side of the veil, it supports us and keeps us going.

People who come through to speak to me often ask their loved ones to move forward and find happiness, as they are just a whisper away, watching and caring for the ones they have left behind. They ask that all bitterness and resentment be dropped and acceptance be found.

It is a privilege—and a huge responsibility—to be a working medium, as you are dealing with people at a very personal level. High levels of compassion and integrity are required, along with a genuine caring and love for all who are experiencing bereavement.

It was a very great pleasure to watch Doris Stokes, the warm and funny British medium, work when she was in Australia many years ago. This lady gave her heart and talents to many people, and she helped them to find a pathway to acceptance. More recently, it was my pleasure to receive readings from Mavis Pitilla and Tony Stockwell, who are both wonderful, humorous, and genuine mediums. I would recommend that grieving people attend a show with a reputable medium—or book a private reading—as the comfort that comes from the other side is incredible.

Mediums are born. Often a person knows from a young age that that they have a strong spiritual connection. They often speak to their guides when they are young and build complete faith and trust in their advice and words of wisdom.

For some the call comes later in life, as they start to work with visions, words, and feelings sent by their spirit guides. There are even times when mediumship comes into being after the death of a loved one.

Mediums are psychic, but psychic readers are not all mediums. There is a need to shift one's consciousness to reach spirit world and to make a link to the one who has passed from this world. Once you have made a link to spirit, you have to hold it while you are relaying the information.

We all work at different levels and awaken in our own time. Wherever you are on your journey, it is a wonderful place to be. Ahead of us all is more learning, honing our skills, improving our clarity, and feeling the wonder from the spirit world.

The information given to the medium is verified by people validating what the medium is saying. It's important for the medium to be accurate with the messages.

The messages are nearly always disjointed, and it is the medium's job to pull it all together so they are giving correct information to the client.

You cannot always predict when the spirit world will reach to link with you and it takes a lot of practise and dedication to be a medium. However it is important to be aware of the difference between a psychic or mediumship reading. Please note that some readings include both energies. I would recommend young mediums join a spiritual circle and work with a teacher on a regular basis for two-three years before reading for the general public.

Case Study

While doing a tarot reading for a young woman, I clearly heard a woman's voice say, "I really don't like her hair that colour." I asked the lady if she had a mother in spirit, and when this was confirmed, I said, "I don't think she likes your hair colour." The young lady laughed and said, "She hated it red, but she's gone now, so I can please myself."

After that point, I passed messages to the daughter that brought her validation and a much-needed time to express her feelings at not being present when her mother passed over. The tarot reading was abandoned, but I think the messages from spirit that day were exactly what the daughter needed to help heal her pain and to move forward into her bright and exciting future.

CHAPTER 40

Spiritual Dictionary

pirit gives us messages in symbolic form, and we are shown pictures that we have to decipher. We have thoughts and feelings—and sometimes brief pain, if we are shown a healing problem. These mind pictures also help us to understand our meditations and dreams.

Psychics may receive many messages. The messages come from their guides or the guides of the people they are reading for. They also come from the auric field of the client.

If I am having trouble getting a *name*, I ask to see someone who has the same name. I have also been shown cartoon characters such as Mickey Mouse and Donald Duck to prompt me in name recognition.

The images and thoughts described below are from my spiritual dictionary, a spiritual reference book I have collated. I hope the descriptions will be of help to you. Enjoy adding to this list and making your own. It is much easier if you are on the same page as your spiritual helper or guide. When you add your own symbols as you work, spirit will honour them.

Spiritual Dictionary

Animal Images

ant. An ant in a reading would refer to a person who works very hard. This person has the energy of the warrior, so you would expect tenacity and strength of character. The person you are reading for may be about to build a house—or maybe a wonderful future with a new partner. The individual would be steadfast and loyal to their family.

ape. An ape is highly intelligent, has strong family bonds, and is very protective. You would be reading for a person who has high family values and is very loving. You could be reading for a shy or emotional person.

buffalo. A buffalo can show an inquisitive person who wants to know the answers to life's questions. A friendly and helpful soul who enjoys having company. Normally powerful and strong, they may at times be very grateful to have someone help them lift burdens.

butterfly. When you see a butterfly, you may be reading for people who have difficulty stilling their minds. They may flit from one idea to another. They like to be entertained, and they have the ability to blend in and mix with a crowd. They love bright colours or unusual clothes and are visually very pleasing. Their emotional state may at times be fragile. They may transform themselves in this lifetime, as they are able to cope with changes. The message in this picture may simply be to tell your client to lighten up and have some fun.

camel. The camel may be in the reading to tell of fluid retention or to warn your client that they are not drinking enough water. The person may be about to embark on a long and arduous trip. If reading for an athlete, the message would be, "Slowly but surely wins the race." The camel doesn't run; it simply picks up the pace. In doing this a camel will retain vital energy that can be used later. Mood swings would be indicated.

cat. This image would refer to a person who is content to laze about, be pampered, and get a lot of attention. This princess persona likes to be pampered and looked after. They are well-presented and may, at times, be telepathic. They can be unpredictable and can suddenly "scratch" others if annoyed, or if things do not go their way. Selfishness may be indicated.

chicken. This animal can be boring—always the same time to bed and the same time to rise. If it refers to the person you are reading for, this person needs a partner who fits into their routine or who at least doesn't mess it up. Self-discipline is likely.

cougar. You could be reading about someone who is looking for a younger lover. Often secretive, this person likes his or her own space. They are usually self-empowered and capable of looking after themselves. The client would enjoy fine things and elegance. They would probably find a good-looking partner and would expect that person to give time and compliments.

cow. Prosperity and comfort is coming to this person. The dark times are over, and there are sunny skies ahead.

dog. The dog image indicates faithfulness from a partner or friends or the ability to be loyal to others. This person may receive accolades for a job well done or for saving a life. They may be a rescuer who enjoys doing things for others.

dolphin. This person may need some healing. They should ask a friend for help or go to a reiki practitioner or other complimentary therapist. It is time for this person to have a holiday with good company, to laugh more, to access personal freedom, to swim, and to cleanse the body. There may be a need for this person to drink more water or to have a bath in Epsom salts to make their aura sparkle. A cruise would be a good idea.

dove. Stress relief is advised. You can advise this stressed individual to be a peacemaker rather than living as a drama queen, always on edge and fighting with others. Suggest that this person put more effort into their current relationship, as it may be starting to fizzle through inactivity. More harmony is needed.

eagle. This indicates that a person may need to step back and have a good look at the situation they are in. They could be too close to see all of the influences. Suggest that they wait for a while before making a life-changing decision and ask for advice from others. This lucky person may be flying somewhere for a holiday.

elephant. Elephants tell us we need strength, stamina, and will power to take us forward. It is time for your client to collect their thoughts and to be definite in opinions and decisions. The elephant image can remind us that we have had this lesson in the past, so it is time to deal with it now. It can also show that a person has the strength needed to overcome an illness. A good friendship is on the way, or there may be an incoming person who will need help and support. Elephants tell us to use our intelligence and intuition to find an answer. They remind us to be assertive when necessary. They also remind us of strength, which comes through having a loving family.

emu. The emu asks us several questions. Are you a sticky beak? Are you over-stretched financially? Do you make unwise comments? Do you pretend to know things that you do not? Are you a gossip? Do you enjoy five minutes of fame by revealing other people's business? Are you sick and tired of being a parent, and are you looking to walk away? Are you about to stick your neck out to help someone who will not appreciate your help?

fox. A situation in which you will need to use cunning is coming up quickly. It is important to keep your thoughts to yourself and watch out for dishonesty around you. Quietly get advice from professionals. You may need to watch out for theft.

fish. This image indicates emotions that may need to be soothed, as the person is going around in circles and getting nowhere fast. This person may be heading into deep water, so they need to take time out and do some more thinking before making a decision. The person you are reading for may be religious, so try not to challenge any long-held belief system.

galah. Someone who is acting childlike or silly is indicated with the galah. It may be the person you are reading for or someone close to them. This person is very noisy, someone who likes parties and group participation. They may become involved in a scandal. Mischief is brewing.

giraffe. This person stands above petty gossip and is sociable and friendly. They have great stamina and move and think fast. They can be disorganized at times. This person likes to have short naps and may suffer from insomnia. This person mixes well with both sexes, but the giraffe could also indicate a homosexual male.

goat. This image indicates enemies, so watch your back. Protect yourself.

hawk. A message of great importance is on the way. Possibly the messenger themselves will have an important impact on your life. Travel will stem from this message.

iguana. This refers to someone who has excellent insight and good outer vision, as well as a unique personality. This person has a need for attention and will stand out in a crowd. They always dare to be different. Caution this person to be patient, as their time is coming.

kitten. This refers to a person who loves to play, someone who is not ready to step up in life and who does not like to make difficult decisions. This child like persona is usually cared for by their parents or older partners. They are cute, want to hear good things, and are very likable.

koala. This image prompts the following questions: Do you feel that this person is being honest with you? Are they hiding from something? Looks can be deceiving, and this person can bark when upset.

leopard. You need time out by yourself to sort out your problems. Meditate to find an answer, as you will need to use cunning and guile to solve a barrier to your journey. Try not to be dogmatic. Be open to new ideas and to positive change.

lion. When a lion enters your head in a reading, it is time to ask the person to act with pride and to stick up for themselves. They may be onto a winning idea, so encourage this person to move forward, as they are underestimating their ability to be steadfast. An award may be coming, and a time of pride and joy is just ahead. If this person feels that they are not being listened to, it is time for them to roar and make their presence felt.

monkey. You are working with a funny person who likes to play tricks and make people laugh. A cheeky person who is great fun to be with. They could also be someone who would make a good actor, as they copy behavior well. They may be bored easily and may not finish what they start.

mouse. A timid person who may miss out on progress, could be represented by the mouse. They will settle for the crumbs rather than stepping up to the mark. It is possible they have small ideas from living a sheltered life, so they like things to stay the same. This image can also warn of property theft.

octopus. This indicates someone who is very sexual and may be a predator. They are too touchy with the opposite sex. Take this as a warning and do not be left alone with someone you do not

241

trust. The image can also warn that the person may have too many irons in the fire and may be overextended.

oxen. The oxen, represents someone who is working too hard and not getting anywhere. However, they are strong and capable and will work until the job is finished. Exhausted, they may be working for someone who is very controlling, leaving them feeling tired and unappreciated. Their efforts may be regularly overlooked. Health problems would include a sore neck and aching shoulders from carrying a heavy burden.

owl. You are not being told all of the truth. Look deeper into a situation, go into meditation, and use wisdom and clarity for the right answer. It might be prudent to get advice from a wise person. Check the legalities: are you being deceived by someone?

panther. The graceful and elegant panther has a very distinct personality. It represents a person who is reliable and protective, one who rarely makes mistakes and would be a good researcher or boss. An energetic person who may dominate in business meetings. They are usually very good at listening.

queen bee. A drama queen is being bought to your attention. You may be dealing with someone in the public eye or someone who needs centre stage and lots of accolades. Expect dramas, manipulation, and controlling behaviour. You could be dealing with someone who is still carrying the energy of the spoilt child. This could also show an affair coming or domestic upheavals.

rhino. This image may indicate that someone who is very thick-skinned is about to make an impression. They will be stubborn and will have tunnel vision. They may be a dangerous enemy.

rooster. Spirit world may be showing you someone who is a braggart, is very sure of themselves, and has a need for attention. Vain and self-centred, this person likes to be heard and may speak loudly.

snake. This image has always warned of an incoming enemy, someone who acts like a snake in the grass, often coming into your home in the guise of a friend. There will definitely be someone like this around you, so be very aware of where you place your trust. The strike will come when you least expect it—in business, on the home front, or in the form of an affair. So watch your back. The snake may also herald illness.

scorpion. This indicates someone who may take their own life, and counselling will be needed in the very near future. Make some positive suggestions and help lift the confidence of someone who is very judgemental of themselves. This image could also indicate a workaholic who is self-destructive or someone who has a "killer" instinct in life and in business.

spider. Diplomacy is required to move forward. Create a good business plan, as there will be an opportunity for advancement through your own endeavours. In the negative, a cunning and manipulative person may be heading your way, weaving a web that you may not be able to get out of. The smallest spider often has the nastiest bite, so watch out for venom from someone unexpected.

tortoise. Moving forward slowly with languid movements, maybe after an illness, means that opportunities may be lost. This person feels tired and takes too long to think things over. They may use a thousand words, when only a hundred are necessary. You could be dealing with closed and heavy boundaries and a person who is not open to good advice. This may also refer to someone who is closed off from love in fear of being hurt.

tadpole. This is the very beginning of something good—a new idea, swimming around without direction—and grounding is required. The tadpole can indicate the start of a new project, with lots of growth to come in the future as new ideas are introduced.

toucan. This image indicates a holiday to an unusual destination or meeting someone from overseas who will become a friend. There may be a connection to Brazil or to someone who lives in Brazil. The toucan suggests a love of nature and time spent relaxing in nature.

unicorn. You need a little magic in your life. You are becoming dull, so step up and try something different. Purity and honesty is needed in a situation. You may have the ability to write fiction books.

wombat. This person runs from trouble but makes slow and steady progress. They feel shy and unsure of themselves, so it is time for them to find a mentor.

wasp. The wasp indicates that someone is sneaking up on you to steal your ideas. It suggests sharp words being spoken and an unexpected sting from a trusted person.

wolf. A good teacher of esoteric studies is coming into your life, and you may become a spiritual teacher in the future. Be humble, treat others well, and earn respect. Always work with honesty and integrity. Wolves love and protect their partners and usually mate for life. Strong lessons are incoming, so be adaptable to positive change, and make sure you are always proud of the decisions you make.

Non-Animal Images

aircraft. New projects or holidays are about to come into your life. Check to see if you have blue or grey skies behind the aircraft. Grey clouds, or a broken wing on the plane, may indicate danger or an accident.

anchor. A voyage is suggested. It is also possible that someone is holding you back from success or personal freedom. The anchor would represent a tired person who feels stuck and needs to move into positive energy.

angels. Healing is needed and is being sent by the angels. The angels advise you to go to the health practitioners for help, as you have an incoming problem that can be resolved. Protection is needed, so take care of your own physical health and that of your family. Lock up your house and car, as something may be stolen. You are receiving love at all times from the angelic worlds, and they are reminding you that you are in a state of grace on earth and that you can create a wonderful new reality. Ask for what you want from the angels, and your dearest wish may come true.

baby. This indicates a possible pregnancy or that someone is acting like a baby by not taking responsibility. It could also mean new ideas, new success, writing a new book, setting up a new business, or just starting out on a new project.

bike. Get on your bike and move on, as exercise is required. You may need to move on from a stale relationship or friendship. Slow down and appreciate the splendour of nature. De-stress by spending time with nature.

bread. This suggests fresh ideas or help from others. A new idea is fermenting, and it will be good. Abundance is on the way.

bride and groom. This image shows soulmates meeting with much joy and love. Engagement and/or marriage is coming for you. Make sure you are both on the same page with your ideas. Discuss important topics before you commit.

Buddah. It's time for reflection. Learn how to meditate, and take time out of your busy life to connect with the inner realms. Patience may be needed in a difficult situation. It might be time to let go of something or someone.

cabin in the woods. Do you need to spend some time with nature? Do you need time out to reflect? This may be a warning not to spend too much money. Stress relief may be a good idea.

cake. This indicates a celebration of a birthday or anniversary, happy family occasions, and sharing happy times.

car. A new car is incoming. A new car can also refer to you and your journey. Look to see if the road is rough or smooth in front of the driver. A holiday may be a good idea. Travel to broaden your mind and your circle of friends.

cup. Is the cup full? If so, you have reached a dream or had success. It may indicate a romance that is progressing well or good times with family and friends. An empty cup means that something is over, and it is time to let go of a situation or person and move on to the next step in your life. Take with you everything you have learned from your last experience, and you will move forward, wiser and ready to start again. Take the skills you have learned into a new job or a new way of life.

clock. Is it time to move forward and leave a job, relationship, or old limiting thought pattern behind? Is time ticking by as you keep saying you will do this, that, or the other *tomorrow*? Is spirit trying to tell you that *now* is the time for you to shine? It is time to make positive changes and spend time with happy people. Spend more time relaxing.

comet. This indicates unexpected happenings, upsets, separation, disappointment, and an overthrowing of a way of life.

flowers.

Daffodils suggest that joy and happiness is coming into the person's life very soon. Good news is on the way. Good times are just around the corner—gifts, gains, and wins.

Pink, red, and magenta gerberas indicate a time to be energetic, happy, and busy, as love and romance are predicted. Ambition and drive are highlighted, with vitality and dreams coming true.

Yellow gerberas indicate that a person is doing a current lesson on setting boundaries and building confidence and self-esteem. A joyful time, right now, with lots of laughter, companionship and self-empowerment. Lots of social times will be coming up, when honesty will be important. Success and achievement are highlighted, fun times with friends and the making of new friends.

Orange and rust-coloured gerberas indicate that creativity is important, as this person is very artistic. They love colour, books, paintings, music, the arts, fine dining, and a good laugh. They can be very sensual. With this person's wicked sense of humour and naughty comments, this person would be very entertaining.

An *iris* would indicate a very spiritual person with high integrity who likes to help others. An important message is coming from spirit world.

Lavender indicates a need to relax and have the soft aroma of lavender around you. You may be too hard on yourself, so take some time out to listen to your inner voice. You may need more sleep. Handle all stressful matters calmly.

The *lily* suggests bereavement. This person is experiencing a difficult time dealing with grief. Tranquillity and serenity are required. Truth is needed to clear up a situation that is worrying the person.

Pansies indicate a soft and gentle person who may have delicate health or may be feeling vulnerable at this time. However, they may have the ability to handle difficult situations with tact and diplomacy.

White roses encourage a person to connect to their spirit guides, spiritual teachers, and higher self for answers—or to talk to their angels. They would be working toward understanding their totality, and with divine inspiration, they would enjoy helping others. Earth healing and healing for humanity is part of this person's journey. They would be open to miracles and would always work with good intent. Spirit gifts are coming their way. Filled with inner harmony, anyone who chooses a white rose is a joy to be with.

Red roses indicate passion, love, energy, and drive. This energetic person may be about to gain a promotion or to propose to their partner. Love and fun times will make this person very happy and complete. A long life would be indicated. The gaining of goals and success is ahead.

Pink roses indicate friendship, feeling cherished, the joy of giving and receiving, and taking delight in the company of loved ones for special anniversaries, birthdays, and fun-filled special times. A warm personality and gentleness is part of this persona.

Mauve roses indicate a strong connection to spirit, along with visions, clairvoyance, clairaudience, and clairsentience. The restructuring of this person's life is in progress. Dream recall and regular meditation will help with spiritual growth. There may be a connection to mother Mary.

Peach or apricot roses indicate a warm and sensual person who enjoys scented candles and oils, soft or fine fabrics, home decorating, artistic endeavours, new and funky clothes, and witty and happy companions. Pregnancy or birth may also be shown here. This person aims for excellence in everything they do. This image can show the start of a new creative project.

fruit.

Apples indicate good health, a healthy romance, or that it is time to go and see one's doctor for a check-up.

Grapes indicate that success is on the way, accolades are coming, and your ambition is about to be rewarded.

Lemons indicate bad news, as someone is acting with bitterness. Therefore they would not be handling a current situation in a positive manner.

grandparents. Wisdom comes from an older person. Giving care to the aged fills your soul. Something from the past is applicable in the future. An inheritance is coming to you soon. A message from spirit will come from a grandparent.

gates. A blockage in the path is to be solved, with the chance to move forward after solving a problem. If this person is open, it will be an easy path ahead; if they are closed, they need to sort out how to be open. Is this person blocking their own pathway with an old, limiting thought pattern?

gatekeeper. This is the spirit person who keeps you safe when you are working with mediumship.

house. The image of a house often refers to the person you are reading for. Is the house a mess? Does it need painting or repairing? Does the garden need attention? What do you see when you walk through the rooms? Whom do you see? Are you looking at a pretty sight that makes your heart sing? Does your house look like it is in good repair? Does it look homey to you and clear of clutter? Is it vibrantly or serenely decorated, depending on which style pleases you? Are there steps up to the house? Are they in good repair? Do you want to stay in your house? Would you like to invite visitors to see your house? Is the garden attractive and inviting? Do you have garden furniture? Take the time to explore and see how you feel about the house and garden. If you are reading for someone else, how do you feel about the way he or she lives or the way they manage their life? Can you give some good advice here? Is there an animal in the garden or an angel or spirit guide?

icicles. This person may be bereaved or grieving over a lost relationship, or they may be cold and unfeeling, judgemental and critical.

invitation. Sometimes you will see an invitation, meaning that the person is going to go somewhere special. How do you feel about this invitation? Will the person be relaxed and enjoy it? Or will they be uncomfortable? Maybe you can give some advice here.

joker. Is this person telling you the truth? Do they have someone around them who consistently lies to them? Are they kidding themselves in a particular situation? Do they have someone around them who acts like a clown? Are they mischievous? Laughter and more time spent having fun would be advised.

junk. It is time to get rid of a lot of old issues. It may be time to move forward, as this person may be stuck in a rut and therefore unable to see the future. If the mess is in the mind, they will lack clarity and grounding. They may be feeling wretched and desolate because they cannot solve their dilemmas.

key. This image indicates prosperity, new guidance, new starts, buying new property, or success for the person you are reading for. The client should be willing to take good advice and to make positive changes. Enlightenment through inner knowledge can possibly be gained through meditation. A new teacher could be working with them in spirit world or in the physical world.

kite. Fly high above the problems. You can win in a situation by rising above your former life to create a new and prosperous one. You need to take time out to play like a child.

ladder. Advancement at work is possible, so this person will be working toward getting a promotion. The ladder also suggests working one's way through spiritual classes and appreciating the results of their endeavours.

lamp. You are about to make an important discovery.

loudspeaker. It is time to step up and be noticed. Consider going to classes for public speaking, so you can learn how to motivate others.

mask. You are hiding from the world for fear of being caught for misdoings. You are not as you appear to be, as you are hiding behind a mask. You may have done something that you know is morally wrong, and you are ashamed of your inappropriate behaviour. You may have a secret lover, or something is being hidden from you. You may be hiding an addiction, in which case you are in need of help from a professional.

mermaid. Allurement is coming your way, and there will be temptation you may not be able to walk away from. The promise of excitement may take you off your path.

musical instrument. Music heals the chakras, so play music, relax, and meditate. Take time to nurture yourself.

necklace. Gifts from someone you admire are coming for you to wear to a special occasion.

obelisk. This refers to a mystical person who is searching for enlightenment and who is trying to reach their true potential. This is someone who has genuine intentions to be the best person they can be. They may be a wisdom-keeper with many secrets hidden in their cells. This could also be making reference to a trip to Egypt.

pen and book. Maybe a future or current author has come to you for sound advice. It could be time to study something new and gain new credentials to help to boost your income.

purse. This indicates incoming money, or maybe you should take care not to lose your purse or have it stolen. This image may also suggest spending money on your home.

pyramid. A trip to a country with pyramids will be in the future for this person. Ancient knowledge will be available to the person at that time. They may also be building a pyramid for success.

pebbles. Small problems will need to be solved. If you are patient, everything will work out okay. Disappointments are just stepping stones to the bigger picture.

rainbow. This is a lucky time in your life, as you will achieve a dream and be successful in all areas of your life. Special gifts are coming, or a windfall is on the way.

rocks. Rocks indicate barriers to your journey and problems to solve before you can continue. The size of the boulders suggests the size of the problems to be worked out. Do you need to be a rock for someone in trouble? Who is the rock in your life?

rays of healing colour.

Red indicates that energy and vitality need to be improved, as the person is very tired.

Orange indicates that creativity may be blocked and fertility may be a problem.

Yellow indicates digestive and stomach problems.

Green indicates that balance and harmony need to be restored for your heart to work fully.

Pink indicates that forgiveness will improve your life, raising the love vibration in your heart.

Blue indicates the healing of physical throat problems. Possibly more tact and diplomacy needs to be introduced.

Mauve helps you to reflect on your life, bringing you into a state of balance.

Indigo indicates that meditation is needed to improve intuition. Try harder to connect to your inner guidance, making friends with your spirit guides.

Violet indicates that cleansing energy is coming your way, encouraging you to let go of bitterness and resentment, anger and fear.

White gives purifying energy to fill your cells and make you feel wonderful as you face the world with enthusiasm and joy.

Turquoise is wonderful for healing the immune system, comforting your inner child, dispelling feelings of abandonment, and helping you to find your inner space.

Silver indicates lots of compassion and empathy for others, as softness and nurturing come with the silver ray. Intuition is heightened.

Gold indicates mental strength, clear thoughts, and good focus, with improved physical stamina.

high heels. This indicates a passionate person who is stepping out for success. This person is sensual and ambitious.

sacred sites. Seeing Machu Picchu, Egyptian pyramids, etc., in your mind's eye indicates that the person will go to these sites, where they may have some past life clearing. Going to this place would enhance the inner power and focus of this person.

sea.

Calm seas indicate that stress relief may come through a holiday by or on the sea to feel at peace and move calmly through life. An opportunity for success will be given.

Crystal-clear water indicates that honesty and integrity are highlighted, with the ability to see the future with clarity and understanding. It refers to the ability to cut through the illusion in one's life and make positive changes.

Rough and or dark seas indicate a refusal to look at the source of your problems and help yourself, as you are looking for someone else to solve your problems. Depression and moodiness might be a concern at his time. You may experience the "poor-me" syndrome or feel ill-at-ease.

Sky-blue seas indicate improvement in communication skills and could suggest talking to and motivating groups.

seaweed. Tangled webs indicate that lies, deceit, and betrayal are heading your way. Stagnant seaweed on the beach shows a refusal to make changes that would be to your benefit. Tangled seaweed around your legs tells you that something you are doing is holding you back. Seaweed floating toward you means that incoming trouble is on the way.

scales of justice. Balance is needed, and you need to be honest in all of your dealings. A lawsuit may be headed your way, so you will need a good lawyer. A good outcome is indicated if you work with the truth.

scissors. A pair of scissors may show the cutting of ties, separation, quarrels, the end of a business partnership, or the end of a marriage. There could be a need to let go of your children and let them leave home.

ship. A ship in the distance may mean a missed opportunity. Something slipped past you, or you may have passed up the opportunity to meet someone who would have played a significant role in your future.

ship sailing away from you. It is time to let go of a past relationship and move forward to create a good future. Let go of old, limiting thought patterns, and create a new and different pathway.

ship coming toward you. Skills you have collected over a lifetime are now about to be used. You now have fresh energy to do new projects, and you will be staying afloat financially. New people are coming into your life, and a soulmate is on the way. Travel may be indicated, with a wonderful holiday to enhance your life. There would be the possibility of a windfall.

rowboat. This is a reminder that pulling together gets results. It may also refer to a feeling that you are in for a long haul with heavy emotions.

six-pointed star. You will be aiming to integrate all aspects and chosen archetypes as you work toward totality. This is the symbol for perfected man and enlightenment.

star. The star is a symbol of hope, often bringing prosperity in all areas of life, along with fame and recognition for hard work. Your dearest wish will come true, as you open to your spiritual gifts.

sunrise. This indicates living in the now and appreciating life's many splendours. If you are starting a new romance, new hopes and dreams will turn into reality.

sunset. This means the end of something and the beginning of something new in your life. You will need to let go of the past and find deep contentment through making wise decisions.

tidal waves. This indicates the overturning of a way of life. Through devastation beyond your control, you will experience major change. Bankruptcy, loss of a job, separation, or death would all be possibilities.

train. Travel over land, taking time out to think things over. Take notice of what is around you as you step out of the driver's seat and just go for the ride.

trees.

> The *oak* tells you to be strong through difficulties and to hold your ground, giving support and shelter to others.
>
> *Palm trees* signify a holiday at the beach or on an island. You are being asked to calm down and enjoy life while you rest and relax in the sunshine.
>
> *Willows* indicate the ability to be flexible in a matter and listen to other points of view, giving you the ability to also give good advice.
>
> *Eucalyptus* indicates that someone from Australia will be playing a role in your near future. Be resilient and have courage and dignity in all situations. Keep your sense of humour, as it will get you through the difficult patches.
>
> *Jacaranda* indicates that you will be working for the highest good of all, connecting to your higher self. You will be open to spiritual guidance, which will raise your vibrations. You will learn how to turn knowledge into wisdom, as you become a powerful spiritual teacher.

weather.

Rain indicates that a cleansing is needed. Something or someone needs to go from your life, as it is time to throw out clutter.

A *storm* indicates that arguments are ahead, with tears and shouting. Trouble and strife have come into your life. Relationships or friendships will break, causing distress and anguish.

A *sunny day* indicates happiness and wonderful times with lovers, family, and friends. Special occasions and anniversaries, birthdays, and the arrival of new babies will bring much joy.

A *cloudy day* indicates arguments with friends, feeling moody or depressed, and not showing appreciation for life. It may suggest that one is not seeing clearly the opportunities that have been presented.

Brilliant sunlight indicates recognition, fame, success, and a time of extreme happiness and personal pride.

Afterword

njoy your journey and be the best you can be.

Try to take some time every day to work through these exercises. The more you do, the quicker you will see the results. Find the passion, the fire within your heart, and utilize it to make some inspired lifestyle changes and to enhance your inner knowing. The exercises are designed to challenge you and to help you to make connections to your spirit guides and inner knowing.

Put aside a little time to meditate. Be aware of the path of your breathing, and in that quiet time, connect to your inner guidance.

People are becoming more and more aware, so step up to the mark in this field and be a role model for honesty, integrity, and exciting change. It is fun to share your journey with a friend or to join a spiritual group. Your greatest asset is a desire to learn and to be genuinely interested in the world of spirit.

Be aware that you may not be successful with every exercise in this book. Some objects that you read and some exercises will be easier for you to work with than others. You may receive a completely different set of information from what I have suggested. Your guides will direct you to the information that is pertinent for your client or for yourself. You are reading possibilities and probabilities, as once you have passed on your findings, the client has free will and can make changes to suit themselves.

Flow with your intuition and remember that my ideas are merely suggestions. They are thoughts for you to start with. Please work without pressure or expectations, be kind to yourself as you enjoy the inner journey. The training methods in this book are designed for you to work with for many years and with much enjoyment.

So follow your dreams, and make your personal development one of your priorities. Be pleasantly surprised by the energy and divine inspiration that will flow through you to assist your learning and to help you support others. If you are learning on your own, choose photographs to read, and spend time sitting in the silence as you connect to your inner knowledge. Record your answers, and you will be thrilled by your progress.

A great sense of humour is one of your best tools for life. As you awaken your own psychic gifts, learn to work with light-heartedness, wisdom, and compassion.

Base your work always on love, divine love, and love for everyone around you. Get motivated. Dive head first into the mysteries of life, and you will develop your prophetic abilities. Let your beautiful spirit range free and listen to the softly spoken whispers. View the colourful images, or simply feel the love and divine light in your body. Spirit connects to us in different ways. It is an incredible privilege to work with these special beings who reach out to give us support and information. I wish for you all a magical life filled with inner harmony, love, light, abundance, prosperity, and success. May you all become successful readers who will continue the journey with wonderful insights and heartfelt compassion.

Glossary

angels. Angels are unique and beautiful beings who come from a lineage different from ours. They take great pleasure in being a support system for the earth experiment. You can speak to them in your meditations or quiet moments. You may like to send them thanks, love, and blessings. They assist with healings and are wonderful protectors for travel or in difficult times.

archangels. There are many archangels. The two I work with are Archangel Michael, who protects me and helps me move through difficult times, and Archangel Rafael, who is a healing angel filled with laughter and compassion.

archetype. An archetype is a model or patterning. We have many archetypal patterns to work from in each incarnation, they serve as guide lines for our behaviour and present us with our lessons. They hold our skills, and abilities and help us to improve through sustained effort. Every archetype which we work with will be a great teacher, and offer many opportunities for spiritual growth. Learning to work with your archetypes, is of great benefit, they teach you not to be a victim, but to take responsibility for your life, and to create the future you would like for yourself.

ascension. Leaving the rounds of karma behind you, move forward to the next step of your journey.

ascended master. One who has completed their journey and has ascended to a higher level to work and to supervise others. This person has gained mastery over themselves.

clairaudience. Clairaudience is the ability to hear spirit. You may hear words, phrases, entire readings, music, or your spirit teacher instructing you. Sometimes the messages are fragmented, and you have to work hard with your spirit dictionary to work out the answers.

clairsentience. Clairsentience is the ability to feel strongly the feelings of others and to be very sensitive to the energy in a room or around people. This is using your heart energy to have empathy and compassion for others. Some people can feel the coming of an earthquake, and others may feel the sorrow of a bereaved person or the happiness emanating from a person in love.

clairvoyance. People who are clairvoyant see images, sometimes like a photograph and sometimes like a movie picture. It is up to you to decode the images or to work with the colours you are being sent.

divine light of spirit. This is the energy that flows from the creator through all of us—everyone and everything. It is responsible for creating our wonderful planet, humans, animals, plants, all of nature, the oceans, seas and rivers, crystals, and the very ground on which we walk.

earth angels. Earth angels are people who step up to the mark and help you in times of crisis or to prevent your untimely death. This is a prearrangement made in spirit before you come to earth.

emotional body. This refers to the astral body where we store our past-life memories and our feelings toward ourselves and others. These emotions form illness in our physical bodies if we do not deal with them. It is a good idea to do some clearing and letting-go exercises so you can move forward in life with enthusiasm and vigour.

future lives. Our future lives are already loosely mapped out. We can make changes to them when planning them in spirit before we come to earth, or we can make changes when we arrive, if we develop spiritually more quickly than expected. It is interesting to look ahead to see what we will be doing in the future. It is encouraging to see if we have moved forward in our thinking and our abilities.

higher self. Our higher self is the overseer of our lives. Nothing is hidden from our higher self, and everything comes back to us through karma. Our higher self tries to help us stay on the path to spiritual enlightenment. The higher self is the overseer of your soul group.

inner light. This refers to the inner light from the threefold flame that resides in our hearts. This light flows through all of us, helping to raise our vibrations.

masters. These are people who have completed their earth journeys and have offered to work with us. They give us answers and encouragement in the dark times. There are many masters, and we work constantly with the masters of the seven rays, but we also acknowledge many others who instruct us, both in our sleep state and in our daily lives.

medium. A medium is a person who links to a spirit or discarnate soul who has passed over from this world. The purpose is to give evidence of life after death and to comfort the bereaved. Mediums work to heal the pain of a bereaved person, passing messages and evidence of life after death from their loved ones.

mediumship. This occurs when an incarnate spirit or earth person communicates with a discarnate spirit who resides in spirit world. Mediumship can be conducted on a one-on-one basis or on a platform where the medium works with the crowd, bringing messages of love and accurate evidence.

monads. These are divine sparks of light that split into twin flames. The twin flames are responsible for the souls groups they send out to learn. Each soul group has a higher self and many personalities. We are all attached to a monad, and we are one of those personalities.

parallel lives. Another aspect of your soul is living another life at the same time you are living this life. The soul divides out to accelerate your learning.

past lives. These are former lives lived by our soul. Our current lives and karma are based on these experiences and played out.

rays. Blue is for power without misuse of power. Yellow is for wisdom. Pink is for divine love and compassion. White is for purity and knowledge. Green is for healing. Ruby is for service. Violet is for forgiveness and transmutation.

soul group. Soul groups are off-shoots from a monad. We all belong to a soul group. Everyone in our soul group is our soulmate.

soulmate. A member of our soul group.

spirit guides. These are souls who are ahead of us on the pathway home. They give their time, energy, and experience to help guide us into making good and moral choices. They are always there to comfort us when we are sad and to cheer for us as we pass our tests. They send unconditional love and do not judge us. When we return to the next dimension, we find that our sprit guides are our friends and teachers in that realm.

telepathy. Telepathy is communicating mind-to-mind with another person. If you work on this exercise, you will improve your connection to spirit, as you will be able to receive messages from them in the same way that you can from a human.

threefold flame. This is the divine threefold flame that resides in our hearts and connects us to the creator. One flame is yellow and represents wisdom; the second is pink and represents unconditional love; and the third is blue, representing our inner power. This flame is small when we start our growth but grows larger as we learn our lessons.

white light. When people leave this plane of existence, they often enter the white light, brilliant and all-encompassing, as they transition into their next state of being. We can also work with white light in our healing sessions to cleanse and rejuvenate.

About the Author

rish was born in Victor Harbour, South Australia, and discovered her gifts at an early age. Her quest has been to pass on her knowledge through her unique ability to teach with passion, humour, and wisdom. Students of all levels are able to resonate with her teaching and be uplifted by her warmth, dedication, and compassion. Trish lives with her husband, Gordon, on the Sunshine Coast of Queensland, Australia. She has two children and seven grandchildren who bring love and laughter into her life.

Trish is a Usui Reiki master/teacher and an Isis Seichim master/teacher. She has diplomas in Corporate Stress Management, Professional Stress Consultancy, and Aromatherapy. She has certificates in Anger and Aggression Management, bereavement counselling and Stress Counselling in the Workplace. Trish is a past-life therapist and tarot reader, and she has spent many years with her guides, learning how to work with psychic and intuitive energy.

Trish takes tours to sacred places to reconnect people to their past skills and to clear trauma from past lives. As an excellent ambassador for the spirit world, Trish also places emphasis on absent healing, global healing, and self-empowerment.

In writing this book, she hopes to encourage people to explore and expand their own gifts. By changing focus and reaching into the silence, it is possible for people to connect to their inner guidance and to improve their reading skills as they work with psychic energy, intuition, clairvoyance, clairsentience, clairaudience, and simply knowing. Trish wants people to enjoy working with the ideas, exercises, and meditations offered in this book and to practice the different methods or readings set out chapter-by-chapter for each person to experience.

Printed by BoD˝in Norderstedt, Germany